Magical
CROCHET

13 Charming Patterns for
Imaginative Crowns, Wings, Unicorns, and More

JEANETTE BØGELUND BENTZEN

SCHIFFER
CRAFT

Other Schiffer Craft Books on Related Subjects:

Fables & Fairy Tales to Cross Stitch: French Charm for Your Stitchwork, Véronique Enginger, ISBN 978-0-7643-5478-6

The Little Guide to Mastering Your Sewing Machine: All the Sewing Basics, Plus 15 Step-by-Step Projects, Sylvie Blondeau, ISBN 978-0-7643-4970-6

Magical Fairy Homes and Gardens, Barbara Purchia and E. Ashley Rooney, Foreword by David D. J. Rau, ISBN 978-0-7643-6745-8

Cover design by Lori Malkin Ehrlich
Layout and illustrations by Jeanette Bøgelund Bentzen
Photography by Sisse Langfeldt, @imagesbylangfeldt, www.imagesbylangfeldt.dk
Product photography by Jeanette Bøgelund Bentzen
Styling by Cæcilie Marie Moustgaard, @moustgaardmodier, www.moustgaardmedier.dk

Type set in Nexa Bold/Light & Minion Pro

ISBN: 978-0-7643-6894-3
Printed in China

Published by Schiffer Craft
An imprint of Schiffer Publishing, Ltd.
4880 Lower Valley Road
Atglen, PA 19310
Phone: (610) 593-1777; Fax: (610) 593-2002
Email: Info@schifferbooks.com
Web: www.schifferbooks.com

For our complete selection of fine books on this and related subjects, please visit our website at www.schifferbooks.com. You may also write for a free catalog.

Schiffer Publishing's titles are available at special discounts for bulk purchases for sales promotions or premiums. Special editions, including personalized covers, corporate imprints, and excerpts, can be created in large quantities for special needs. For more information, contact the publisher.

We are always looking for people to write books on new and related subjects. If you have an idea for a book, please contact us at proposals@schifferbooks.com.

CONTENTS

PROJECTS

INTRODUCTION

This book includes 13 patterns for crocheted rainbows, unicorns, and other fantasies in a lovely mixture of practical, decorative, and, of course, playful designs.

The book's universe is deeply inspired by my dear daughter, Selma, who is three years old. I know well that look in her eyes when she sees something with a hint of glitter. I can remember how I felt when I first saw her seduced by glimmering details and beautiful colors. She went with the flow and disappeared into an adventurous universe, one created with her own limitless and fantastic imagination. I've also visited that world, letting myself fall into it and play along.

Play is so important, so I kept it front of mind when designing the projects in this book. I've made an effort to incorporate magical details and beautiful finishing in every piece. I approached the designs using a solid set of crochet basics, and everything was created with a quiet Nordic vibe—but with loads of glitter, of course!

For some of the designs, the details take as much time as the crocheting itself, and that is totally okay. It's the love, thoroughness, and play that you put into a piece that gives it that extra-special something. If you approach the projects with patience and summon up your inner child, I'm sure you'll enjoy the making process as much as I have. Allow yourself to use your imagination when choosing beads and embroidering beautiful motifs in delightful color combinations and glitter yarn—and see where it takes you. I hope that when you crochet the items in this book you can let yourself enjoy the same adventurous sense of play that your little ones will experience from the finished items.

THE DETAILS

When it comes to crochet design, I am a nerd with nerd tendencies: I love digging into details and trying to optimize and refine as much as I can. In some places, this means that a pattern might seem more convoluted or difficult compared to what you may have expected at first.

So, I want to remind you that the patterns are only suggestions, and you should do as you prefer in your own way—the way you find easiest and smoothest. By no means should you give up or get discouraged.

If you find an increase or decrease in a pattern that you think is annoying or a method of changing colors that you don't completely understand, just ignore those details. Remember, they are only details!

GENERAL INFORMATION, TIPS, AND TRICKS

CROCHET HOOKS

I need to preach for a moment about crochet hooks, because the type of hook you use can make a big difference—to the end result and to the amount of pleasure you get while crocheting.

If you're crocheting a rug with heavy yarn, perhaps in a granny stripe or similar pattern, the type of hook you use won't make a big difference. However, most of the designs in this book are worked with a small crochet hook, and if you want a relatively firm structure, you *will* really notice a difference depending on your hook. So, I highly recommend using crochet hooks by Clover Amour or Clover Soft Touch. The primary differences between these two are the shafts and the lengths of the metal sections. The heads have the same shape. Both have a good coating.

This recommendation is based on my many hours of crochet experience as well as observations and chats I've had with participants in my workshops. Paying a little more for a really good crochet hook is worth it, considering that it's your primary tool and that you'll use it for many years, if not the rest of your life.

HOOK SHAFT

Most makers choose crochet hooks based on a shaft that feels comfortable, and many people believe that the shaft is the primary factor for avoiding "slide" in their hands. The shaft is of course important. But there are also other, more significant factors to consider, at least in my experience. Read on!

HOOK HEAD

One important factor to consider is the size and shape of the hook head. If you have a crochet hook with a very round and slightly large hook head, it can be quite difficult to insert the hook through the stitches, especially if you want to crochet a piece with a firm structure.

HOOK COATING

A second, often-overlooked, important factor is the hook coating on the metal, which can make the yarn slide much more easily. When you combine a relatively pointed hook head with a nicely coated hook, you can achieve a much faster result with less effort.

CHANGING CROCHET HOOKS

Keep in mind that when you change to new crochet hooks, it will take a little patience and adjustment at first, as you recalibrate your fine motor skills. I began crocheting with Clover Soft Touch but later switched to Clover Amour. Despite the fact that they're relatively similar, I needed a period of adjustment before I was once again working happily and had regained my usual speed.

YARN

If you haven't worked with glittery, shiny, or sparkly yarn before, you're in for a treat! All the photos in this book show yarn from Krea Deluxe, which has an unbelievably beautiful and soft color palette with many shades within the same color group.

The following types of yarn are used:

Organic Cotton *(100% organic cotton).* **180 yd (165 m) per 50 g.**

Organic Wool 2 *(100% organic Merino wool).* **93 yd (85 m) per 50 g.**

Shiny *(80% viscose, 20% polyester).* **104 yd (95 m) per 25 g.**

As always, when you choose to substitute yarns, take care to match them to the project's specified weights to avoid any gauge problems. Because I recommend ironing or dampening the pieces for several of the designs, you should be careful to check the fibers in any substitute yarn you have chosen. You also need to make sure that the yarn can tolerate heat, so avoid acrylic. If there's any doubt, test your yarn.

Some options for the **Organic Cotton** include:

Hobbii: Rainbow Deluxe 8/4 *(100% Turkish cotton).* 186 yd (170 m) per 50 g.

Hobbii: Rainbow 8/4 *(100% cotton).* 186 yd (170 m) per 50 g.

Hobbii: Baby Cotton Organic *(100% Egyptian cotton).* 185 yd (170 m) per 50 g.

Hobbii: Friends Cotton *(100% mercerized cotton).* 74 yd (160 m) per 50 g.

Hobbii: Baby Cotton Organic Mercerized *(100% Egyptian cotton).* 185 yd (170 m) per 50 g.

Paintbox Yarns: Cotton 4-ply *(100% cotton).* 186 yd (170 m) per 50 g.

Cotton Kings: Cotton 8/4 *(100% cotton).* 186 yd (170 m) per 50 g.

Some options for the **Organic Wool 2** include:

Mayflower: Easy Care Big *(100% superwash Merino wool).* 93 yd (85m) per 50 g.

BC: Semilla Grosso GOTS *(100% superwash wool).* 87 yd (80m) per 50 g.

Hobbii: Friends Wool *(100% wool).* 109 yd (100 m) per 50 g.

Hobbii: Tweed Delight *(85% wool, 10% acrylic, 5% viscose).* 109 yd (100 m) per 50 g.

Hobbii: Umami Tweed *(75% acrylic, 22% wool, 3% viscose).* 90 yd (83 m) per 50 g.

Cascade Yarns: ReVive *(100% wool).* 197 yd (180 m) per 100 g.

Lion Brand Yarn: Local Grown *(100% wool).* 186 yd (170 m) per 100 g.

Some options for the **Shiny** include:

Go Deluxe: Cocktail Deluxe *(100% polyester).* 98 yd (90 m) per 25 g.

Hobbi: Twister Glitter *(53% cotton, 43% acrylic, 4% metallic).* 1,093 yds (1,000 m) per 250 g.

Lion Brand Yarn: Bonbons Metallic *(96% acrylic, 4% metallic).* 38 yd (35 m) per 10 g.

BEADS, ELASTIC, AND RIBBONS

I encourage you to begin or expand your collection of small beads, buttons, elastic, and ribbons. You can buy them in fabric shops, hobby stores, and yarn shops as well as from various online shops. I also recommend looking in secondhand stores, where you might be lucky enough to find something exciting.

SAFETY

Be careful to sew beads and buttons on very securely. Always consider whether a child who may be in contact with an item is old enough that beads and similar items won't constitute a danger. It's always an option to embroider French knots instead of beads or to crochet bobbles or something similar.

The same cautions apply regarding the length of any cords, tie bands, and elastic. For example, when making the Play Crown, instead of using tie bands, you could sew a short length of wide elastic from one side to the other.

EMBROIDERY

For the embroidery in this book, I used the same yarns as for the crocheting: Organic Cotton or Shiny. Because these are not embroidery yarns, you may experience some difficulty in getting a uniform result. When you embroider with Organic Cotton, your cross stitches might be relatively thin at the beginning, but will widen as you practice, in step with the yarn plies, as they begin to divide and become fuller. I recommend that you begin by separating the yarn into four individual strands, even if that takes a bit of time. Or you can use regular embroidery thread, which behaves and lays down differently and makes it easier to obtain a more uniform result.

FABRIC, FUSIBLE INTERLINING, AND INTERFACING

Some of the projects in this book use fabric, fusible interlining, and/or interfacing. I describe each of these below and which designs they are used in. (You'll find the how-to details in each project's instructions.) I chose these materials so you can make all the designs without a sewing machine.

FABRIC

I recommend using fabric that is firmly woven and not too stretchy, so it will be easier to iron. It should also tolerate a certain amount of heat to allow, for instance, iron-on interfacing. Fabric is used for the wrong side of the Play Wings.

FUSIBLE INTERLINING

Iron-on interlining is available in several weights and for various uses. For these patterns, I used a stiff interlining (*Vlieseline H 250*) that has one glue side. It is ironed on to stiffen the piece and lock in its shape. It is used for the Play Crown and Play Wings.

DOUBLE-SIDED FUSIBLE INTERFACING

Two-sided fusible interfacing has glue on both sides, one of which is protected by paper. Its glue side 1 is first ironed onto the textile, such as crocheted fabric. Then, the peel-off paper is removed so glue side 2 can be ironed onto the fabric. I used the brand Vliesofix for affixing fabric to the wrong side of the Play Wings.

DAMPENING AND IRONING

Take the effort to dampen or iron your work to block it, even during the making process. For most designs, it makes a noticeable difference. Crocheted fibers are easily reshaped, and you can help the stitches even out as you manipulate the piece a bit, so that, for example, a circle becomes even rounder.

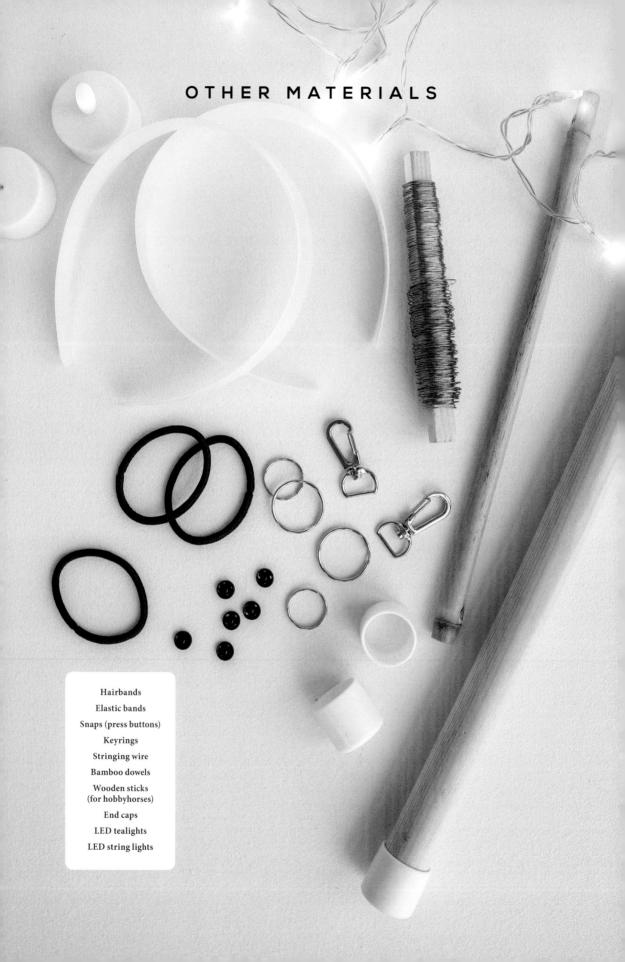

OTHER MATERIALS

Hairbands

Elastic bands

Snaps (press buttons)

Keyrings

Stringing wire

Bamboo dowels

Wooden sticks
(for hobbyhorses)

End caps

LED tealights

LED string lights

HOW TO READ THE PATTERNS

Before you begin working, first read the pattern all the way through so you'll have an overview of the instructions.

GRAY PARENTHESES (...)

The number(s) within gray parentheses indicate how many stitches you will end up with at the end of a row or round. This is not the total number of stitches you have crocheted, but rather the number of stitches you can count on a round or row when you've completed it.

Example 1

Rnd 2: 1 sc in each st (12).

This is an ordinary round with 1 single crochet stitch worked in each stitch of the previous round, and you have 12 stitches per round at the end = (12).

Example 2

Rnds 3–4: 1 sc in each st (12).

Here, you work several rounds with 1 single crochet stitch worked in each stitch of the previous round. If, for example, there are two rounds, as in the example here, you will work a total of 24 stitches, but the number of stitches at the end of the round, when you have completed it and count, is still just 12 stitches = (12).

Example 3

Rnd 5: 6 x [1 sc, 1 Iinc], 1 sc (*to shift beginning of rnd here and for rest of pattern*) (18).

This example shows a single round with invisible increases that ends with an extra single crochet to shift the beginning of the following round. You will have crocheted a total of 19 stitches, but, when you are finished and count, there are still only 18 stitches on the round = (18).

BRACKETS [...]

The stitches framed by brackets should be repeated a certain number of times as indicated before the opening bracket.

Example

Rnd 3: 6 x [2 sc, 1 inc]

The sequence within brackets should be repeated 6 times. Below, you can see how it would look if it was completely written out.

Rnd 3: 2 sc, 1 inc, 2 sc, 1 inc, 2 sc, 1 inc, 2 sc, 1 inc, 2 sc, 1 inc, 2 sc, 1 inc

ASTERISKS *...*

The stitches or sequence between asterisks should be repeated around. I use asterisks primarily in places where the sizes vary; for example, for the tealight lanterns.

Example

Rnd 24: *3 sc, ch 3, skip next 3 sts*

For this example, the round has 18 stitches, so the steps within asterisks are to be repeated 3 times. Below, you can see how it would look if it was completely written out.

Rnd 24: 3 sc, ch 3, skip next 3 sts, 3 sc, ch 3, skip next 3 sts, 3 sc, ch 3, skip next 3 sts

VIDEOS

This QR code links to a playlist on my YouTube channel where you'll find instructional videos on some of the techniques used in the book. The playlist is called "Magical Crochet."

You'll find these videos included in the playlist:

Bobble stitch

Joining beginning of round

Color changes with stripes

Crochet cord

Crab stitch

Magic ring

Sharp color change

Invisible decrease with single crochet

Invisible increase with single crochet

Slip knot

Long single crochet stitch

Making an invisible finishing join

X-sc versus Y-sc

WHAT YOU SEE IN THE PICTURES

Please note that the patterns were adjusted and corrected as they were worked through, and also sometimes in response to feedback from test crocheters. Therefore, some of the projects you see in the photos are not necessarily identical to the patterns themselves. This means that you can't use the pictures to count stitches and rows, for example. We're talking about small adjustments; the overall look of your creation will, of course, be the same, perhaps just a bit more refined. One example is the Backpack, where there is an extra "hole" included in the structure to make it more symmetrical overall.

ABBREVIATIONS AND TECHNIQUES

NOTE TO READERS

You may want to bookmark this section for reference as you work, because some of the techniques used are less common variations on typical crochet stitches. Make sure you have read and understand the instructions before getting started.

ABBREVIATIONS

bl	back loop
ch	chain stitch
ch lp	chain loop
CR	close round
dc	double crochet (= British treble crochet)
dec	decrease
hdc	half double crochet (= British half treble crochet)
Idec	invisible decrease
Iinc	invisible increase
inc	increase
Lsc	long single crochet
rem	remain(s)(ing)
rnd(s)	round(s)
RS	right side
sc	single crochet (= British double crochet)
SCC	stripe color change
ShCC	sharp color change
sl st	slip stitch
st(s)	stitch(es)
WS	wrong side
X-sc	X-single crochet
Y-sc	Y-single crochet

Two different types of single crochet are used in this book. I describe each below. Make sure you note which one to work in each case.

Y-SINGLE CROCHET

Single crochet in which the yarn goes over the hook

(*This method is the most common and standard method, the one considered to be typical single crochet.*)

Insert the hook in under both stitch loops, yarn over hook (*hook goes under yarn*), bring yarn through so you have two loops on the hook, yarn over hook (*hook goes under yarn*), and bring yarn through both loops.

This is the most common method of working a single crochet, and, for most cases, also the quickest. If there is no Y or X listed, work a single crochet in which the yarn goes over the hook as described here. This also applies when you make other crochet stitches. It is very important that the yarn goes over the hook when you work long single crochet stitches, to avoid crossing the legs of the stitch.

X-SINGLE CROCHET

Single crochet in which the hook goes over the yarn in the first half of the stitch

Insert the hook under both stitch loops, yarn UNDER hook (*hook goes OVER the yarn*), bring yarn through so you have two loops on the hook, yarn over hook (*here the hook goes under the yarn as usual and not over the yarn as in the first pass*), and bring yarn through both loops.

This type of single crochet stitch takes a bit more time to work and might seem a little unnatural or troublesome for your hand. So, it's used only in those places where I think it is worth the effort.

There are mainly two circumstances where I chose this type of single crochet in some patterns.

The first scenario is when working single crochet in the round where the stitches will be embroidered on later. With this type of single crochet, the rounds do not bias to the same degree as for normal Y-single crochet stitches, and you will often only need to finish by steaming the work so the stitches will lie neatly over each other.

The second scenario is when you want to make a firm structure. You can do so with this type of single crochet, and it is ideal for items such as a teddy bear that will have filling added in at the end.

DECREASES AND INCREASES

(X- or Y-single crochet stitches, as stated in the pattern instructions)

DEC = DECREASE(S) = NORMAL DECREASE METHOD

Crochet 2 single crochet stitches together.

Insert hook under both stitch loops on the first stitch, yarn over hook and bring yarn through so you now have two loops on the hook. Insert hook under both stitch loops on next stitch, yarn over hook and bring yarn through so you now have three loops on the hook. Yarn over hook and bring yarn through all three loops.

iDEC = INVISIBLE DECREASE

Insert hook under front loop of first stitch, then insert hook under front loop of second stitch and work as 1 single crochet.

INC = INCREASE(S) = NORMAL INCREASE METHOD

Work 2 single crochet stitches into the same stitch (*inserting hook under both stitch loops*).

iINC = INVISIBLE INCREASE

First, work 1 single crochet stitch into back loop of the stitch. Then work 1 single crochet stitch into both loops of the same stitch.

CHANGING COLORS

ShCC = SHARP COLOR CHANGE

The stitch before the color change (the last stitch of the original color) is finished with the new color.

SCC = STRIPE COLOR CHANGE

(at the new color in stripes)

The color change is made as follows, when you have finished with the last stitch before the color change:

- Make the loop on the hook a little larger, remove hook from loop, and let loop hang.
- Insert hook from the wrong side in under both loops of first stitch of round. Place the hanging loop back onto hook and bring loop with it to wrong side.
- Now catch the new color, bring it through the loop, and chain 1. Tighten yarn of hanging color as well as the loose yarn end of new color.
- Continue crocheting with the new color. Don't forget, when beginning the next round, the first stitch of the round is worked into the same stitch, where you brought the loop through to the wrong side for the color change.

CR = CLOSE ROUND

(at the first stripe after a color change)

In principle, this is the same technique as for the color change in stripes—but here you omit the color change. This method of connecting rounds is used on the first round after a color change as you continue with the same color.

This means that the rounds are joined smoothly. If you then work with the same color, you will be working in a spiral.

The round is joined as follows, when the last stitch of the round is worked:

- Make the loop on the hook a little larger, remove hook from loop, and let loop hang.
- Insert hook from the wrong side in under both loops of first stitch of round. Place the hanging loop back onto hook and bring loop with it to wrong side.
- Chain 1.
- Continue crocheting. Don't forget, when beginning the next round, the first stitch of the round is worked into the same stitch, where you brought the loop through to the wrong side at a color change.

MISCELLANEOUS

SLIP KNOT

This is just the first knot or loop you form when you, for example, want to begin chain stitches.

CROCHETING IN A SPIRAL

If you crochet in the round without beginning or ending the round with a chain or slip stitch, the work will continue in a spiral.

MAKING AN INVISIBLE FINISHING JOIN

- When you've worked the last stitch of a round *(no matter if the round consists of single crochet or slip stitches)*, cut yarn and pull yarn tail through last stitch.
- Thread this yarn tail into a tapestry needle.
- Insert the tapestry needle through the front of the first stitch of the last round, through both loops and pull through. Next, insert the needle through the back loop of the last stitch made.

lSC = LONG SINGLE CROCHET

A long single crochet is, in principle, worked like a normal single crochet, but, instead of inserting the hook in under the stitch loops of the next stitch as normal, the hook is inserted one or several rows below that. Additionally, you can work long single crochet on the bias; you can, for example, insert the hook into a stitch to the right, two rows down.

Insert the hook into the correct stitch loops (*as instructed in pattern*), yarn over hook, bring yarn through and stretch up to appropriate height so you have 2 loops on the hook (make sure the loop is not too tight), yarn over hook, and pull through both loops on hook. If the legs of the stitch get twisted, you can readjust them later.

BOBBLES

A bobble is, in principle, 4 half-finished double crochet stitches that are then joined. They are always worked on the wrong side so they will naturally "bobble" out on the opposite side of the one you are working on.

- Yarn over hook, insert hook under both loops of next stitch, yarn over hook, and bring yarn through so you have 3 loops on the hook. Yarn over hook and bring through 2 loops; 2 loops remain on hook.
- Repeat the previous step three more times, all into the same stitch, so you end up with a total of 5 loops on the hook.
- Finally, yarn over hook and bring yarn through all 5 loops at once.
- Work 1 single crochet in the following stitch.
- If you are working several bobbles, one after the other, don't forget to always work 1 single crochet between each bobble.

CRAB STITCH

A crab stitch is worked like a single crochet, but toward the right in the round, or backward, instead of working leftward around as is normal.

MAGIC RING

Make a small circle of yarn, with the loose yarn end hanging at the left and beneath the yarn end coming from the ball. Insert hook through the top of the circle, catch the ball yarn and bring it through the ring; yarn over hook and pull through the loop on the hook. Continue crocheting around the ring, making as many single crochet stitches as specified in pattern. Once you've completed the initial round of stitches, pull the loose yarn end to close up the circle.

SEWING AND EMBROIDERY

OVERHAND STITCH

Sew along an outer edge without pulling the yarn/thread too tightly. Sew from right to left.

DOUBLE RUNNING STITCH

This stitch is sewn back and forth (*the stitches form a straight line—they should be equal in length on the front and back of the fabric*). This stitch can also be made as a backstitch, but that might be difficult if the material is thick (*for example, through two layers of elastic*).

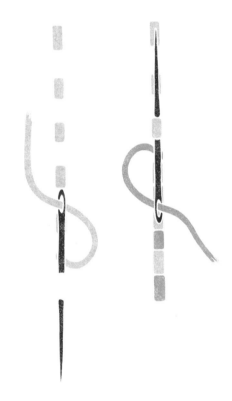

CROSS STITCH

A cross stitch consists of an under stitch, sewn from left to right, and an over stitch, sewn from right to left. The completed stitch makes a cross on the right side of the work.

Sew the stitches from the top down—first a whole row of under stitches, and then a whole row of over stitches crossing the under stitches. You can also work complete cross stitches one at a time if you prefer.

RAINBOWS AND COLOR CHOICES

Here are some suggestions for color combinations and progressions (the color codes shown here are for Organic Cotton yarn from Krea Deluxe).

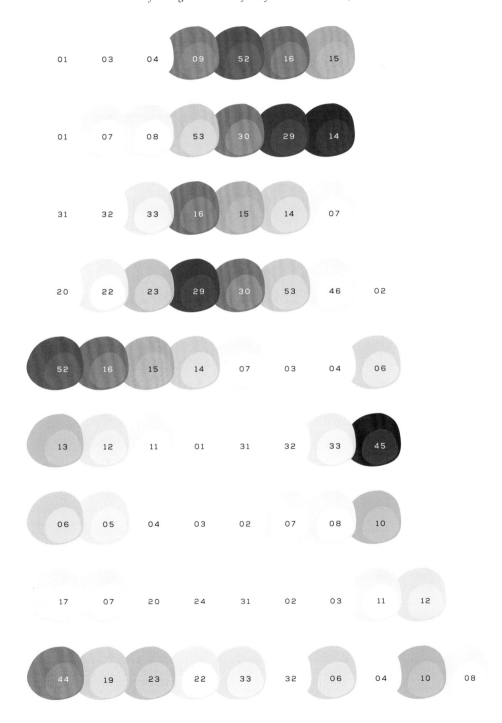

01   03   04   09   52   16   15

01   07   08   53   30   29   14

31   32   33   16   15   14   07

20   22   23   29   30   53   46   02

52   16   15   14   07   03   04   06

13   12   11   01   31   32   33   45

06   05   04   03   02   07   08   10

17   07   20   24   31   02   03   11   12

44   19   23   22   33   32   06   04   10   08

PROJECTS

HAIRBAND

Here's a basic pattern for a versatile hairband that works for everyday wear, for parties, or for playtime. Make it unique by adding stripes, sew on beads for a party version, or go all out and sew on a unicorn horn and ears.

SIZES	One size
CROCHET HOOK	U.S. D-3 (3 mm)
YARN	Color A: 25 g Organic Cotton If adding a horn: Color B: small amount (4–5 g) Shiny
NOTIONS	• Hairband, 9¾ in (25 mm) (*the hairband used for this project is narrow at the ends and wider toward the middle*) • Small amount of fiberfill for the horn (if you're making the unicorn version) • Beads (if you're making the beaded version)
GAUGE	Gauge is not important here, but it is important that the fabric is relatively firm and fits over the hairband. Use a half or whole size larger or smaller hook to adjust the gauge so the pieces will fit your hairband.
CONSTRUCTION	• The hairband is narrow at the ends and wider toward the center. The cover is crocheted in two pieces, each worked in the round and then sewn together at the middle. This makes it easier to pull on than if you crochet all around the hairband. • You can embellish the band with beads or other decorative elements. • If you are making the unicorn version, crochet the horn and ears and then sew them on last.

2 X HAIRBAND PIECES

NOTES

- All single crochet stitches are Y-single crochet stitches.
- Each piece is worked in a spiral.
- If you want to make stripes, see page 30 for five stripe sequence options.

Color A

Rnd 1: Make a magic ring and work 6 sc around it (6).

Rnd 2: 2 x [1 Iinc, 2 sc] (8).

Rnds 3–9: 1 sc in each st around (8).

Work 2 sc (*to shift beginning of rnd here and for rest of pattern*).

Rnd 10: 1 Iinc, 7 sc (9).

Rnds 11–17: 1 sc in each st around (9).

Work 2 sc.

Rnd 18: 1 Iinc, 8 sc (10).

Rnds 19–25: 1 sc in each st around (10).

Work 2 sc.

Rnd 26: 1 Iinc, 9 sc (11).

Rnds 27–33: 1 sc in each st around (11).

Work 2 sc.

Rnd 34: 1 Iinc, 10 sc (12).

Rnds 35–41: 1 sc in each st around (12).

Work 2 sc.

Rnd 42: 1 Iinc, 11 sc (13).

Rnds 43–49: 1 sc in each st around (13).

Work 2 sc.

Cut yarn and fasten off, leaving a long end for seaming.

HAIRBAND CHART

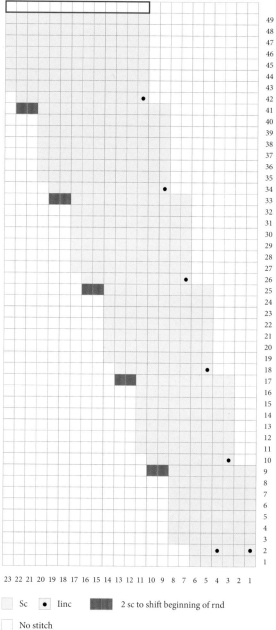

Sc • Iinc ▓▓ 2 sc to shift beginning of rnd

☐ No stitch

☐ This round is the join
(*used if you want to place stripes symmetrically*).

FINISHING

- Place the two pieces on the hairband, making sure that you hide the increases on the inside of the band.

- Seam the two ends.

- Thread the two yarn ends into a tapestry needle and sew the two pieces together with overhand stitch all around. Make sure the seam is tight.

- Weave in ends.

SUGGESTIONS FOR STRIPE SEQUENCE

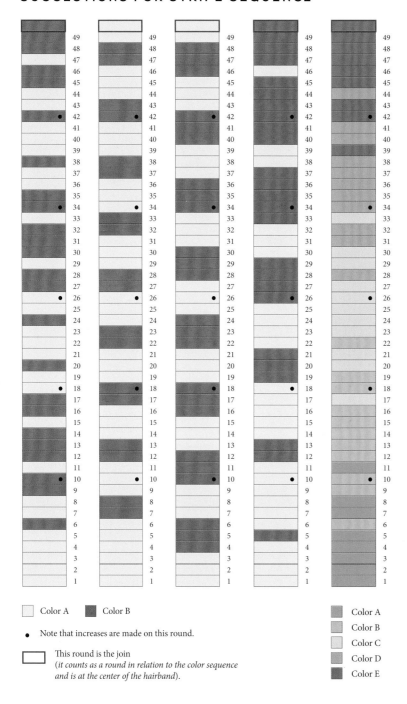

Color A   Color B

- Note that increases are made on this round.

This round is the join
(*it counts as a round in relation to the color sequence
and is at the center of the hairband*).

Color A
Color B
Color C
Color D
Color E

EARS CHART

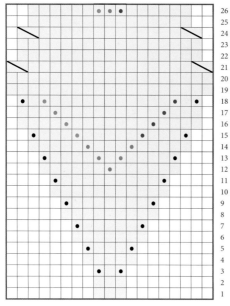

26
25
24
23
22
21
20
19
18
17
16
15
14
13
12
11
10
9
8
7
6
5
4
3
2
1

19 18 17 16 15 14 13 12 11 10 9 8 7 6 5 4 3 2 1

	Sc
•	Iinc
⟋	Idec
	Repeat once more

EMBROIDERY

Embroider from the lowest 3 points/ stitches on the ear to each of the other points/stitches in the corresponding color.

2 X EARS

The ears are crocheted in the round from the tip down. They are finished with embroidery in an optional contrast color.

NOTES

- All single crochet stitches are worked as X-single crochet.
- Each piece is worked in a spiral.

Color A

Rnd 1: Make a magic ring and work 6 sc around it (6).

Rnd 2: Work 1 sc in each st around (6).

Rnd 3: 2 x [1 Iinc, 1 sc, 1 Iinc] (10).

Rnd 4: Work 1 sc in each st around (10).

Rnd 5: 2 x [1 Iinc, 3 sc, 1 Iinc] (14).

Rnd 6: Work 1 sc in each st around (14).

Rnd 7: 2 x [1 Iinc, 5 sc, 1 Iinc] (18).

Rnd 8: Work 1 sc in each st around (18).

Rnd 9: 2 x [1 Iinc, 7 sc, 1 Iinc] (22).

Rnd 10: Work 1 sc in each st around (22).

Rnd 11: 2 x [1 Iinc, 9 sc, 1 Iinc] (26).

Rnd 12: Work 1 sc in each st around (26).

Rnd 13: 2 x [1 Iinc, 11 sc, 1 Iinc] (30).

Rnd 14: Work 1 sc in each st around (30).

Rnd 15: 2 x [1 Iinc, 13 sc, 1 Iinc] (34).

Rnds 16–17: Work 1 sc in each st around (34).

Rnd 18: 2 x [1 Iinc, 15 sc, 1 Iinc] (38).

Rnds 19–20: Work 1 sc in each st around (38).

Rnd 21: 2 x [1 Idec, 15 sc, 1 Idec] (34).

Rnds 22–23: Work 1 sc in each st around (34).

Rnd 24: 2 x [1 Idec, 13 sc, 1 Idec] (30).

Rnds 25–26: Work 1 sc in each st around (30).

Cut yarn. Fasten off, leaving an end long enough for sewing ear together and for attaching to hairband.

FINISHING

- Embroider inside of ears with color B. Cut yarn, fasten off, and weave in ends on WS.
- Lay ears flat and sew together.
- Fold each side of ear in toward center and sew together.
- Finally, sew each ear to hairband.

HORN

The horn is worked in a spiral, however it is not worked in traditional rounds. The last stitch will be moving and adjusting—more freeform, so you will be working some of the last stitches of a round into the next round. The last stitch you work will not always be on top of your last round's last stitch. In a way similar to a shift stitch, you will adjust the last stitch for these rounds.

NOTES

- All single crochet stitches are worked as X-single crochet.
- Each piece is worked in a spiral.
- Don't forget to add fiberfill several times while making the horn.

TIPS

I recommend that you note down each time you have worked a round so you know how far you've come. When the rounds are crocheted "over themselves," it can be very difficult to "see" glitter yarn stitches, whether there are decreases or increases, as well as when counting backward.

Be especially careful when working invisible decreases at the end of each round, because the stitches can be "drawn in" and can easily trick your eye so it looks like there is an extra stitch when you count. You might, as a result, begin the next round too soon (*that is, in the same stitch as the last stitch, where you made the decrease*).

Color B

Rnd 1: Make a magic ring and work 5 sc around it (5).

Rnd 2: Work 1 sc in each st around (5).

Rnd 3: 1 Iinc, 4 sc (6).

Rnd 4: 1 sc, 2 Iinc, 2 sc, 1 Idec (7).

Rnd 5: 4 sc, 1 Iinc, 2 sc, 1 Idec (7).

Add a little fiberfill. From this point on, I recommend you add fiberfill after every other round.

Rnd 6: 3 sc, 2 Iinc, 2 sc, 1 Idec (8).

Rnd 7: 5 sc, 1 Iinc, 2 sc, 1 Idec (8).

Rnd 8: 4 sc, 2 Iinc, 2 sc, 1 Idec (9).

Rnd 9: 6 sc, 1 Iinc, 2 sc, 1 Idec (9).

Rnd 10: 5 sc, 2 Iinc, 2 sc, 1 Idec (10).

Rnd 11: 7 sc, 1 Iinc, 2 sc, 1 Idec (10).

Rnd 12: 6 sc, 2 Iinc, 2 sc, 1 Idec (11).

Rnd 13: 8 sc, 1 Iinc, 2 sc, 1 Idec (11).

Rnd 14: 7 sc, 2 Iinc, 2 sc, 1 Idec (12).

Rnd 15: 9 sc, 1 Iinc, 2 sc, 1 Idec (12).

Rnd 16: 8 sc, 2 Iinc, 2 sc, 1 Idec (13).

Rnd 17: 10 sc, 1 Iinc, 2 sc, 1 Idec (13).

Rnd 18: 9 sc, 2 Iinc, 2 sc, 1 Idec (14).

Rnd 19: 11 sc, 1 Iinc, 2 sc, 1 Idec (14).

Rnd 20: 10 sc, 2 Iinc, 2 sc, 1 Idec (15).

Rnd 21: 12 sc, 1 Iinc, 2 sc, 1 Idec (15).

Rnd 22: 11 sc, 2 Iinc, 2 sc, 1 Idec (16).

Rnd 23: 13 sc, 1 Iinc, 2 sc, 1 Idec (16).

Rnd 24: 12 sc, 2 Iinc, 2 sc, 1 Idec (17).

Rnd 25: 14 sc, 1 Iinc, 2 sc, 1 Idec (17).

Rnd 26: 13 sc, 2 Iinc, 2 sc, 1 Idec (18).

Rnd 27: 15 sc, 1 Iinc, 2 sc, 1 Idec (18).

Rnd 28: 14 sc, 2 Iinc, 2 sc, 1 Idec (19).

Rnd 29: 16 sc, 1 Iinc, 2 sc, 1 Idec (19).

Rnd 30: 1 sc in each st around (19).

The horn should now be about 4 in (10 cm) high.

Cut yarn and fasten off, leaving an end long enough for sewing horn securely to hairband.

FINISHING

- Sew horn securely onto hairband.
- Weave in all ends neatly on WS.

MAGIC WAND

You can't make magic without a magic wand. Just remember to tell your child that they shouldn't turn anyone into a frog.

This project is designed to use up leftovers. There are two different versions of the circles for you to choose from. The first version has color changes and long single crochet stitches to create a wonderful toy, and it can be a fun challenge. The other version is a single color and is easy for anyone, and you can decorate it with embroidery and beads.

SIZES	One size
CROCHET HOOK	U.S. D-3 (3 mm)
YARN	Color A: small amount of Organic Cotton Color B: small amount of Organic Cotton Color C: small amount of Organic Cotton Color D: 25 g Organic Cotton Color E: small amount of Shiny
NOTIONS	• Bamboo dowel or something similar, about ¼ in (7–8 mm) in diameter and 9¾–10¼ in (25–26 cm) long • Sandpaper: if you are cutting a stick you found outside, use this to smooth the ends • Fiberfill for the star
GAUGE	Gauge is not important here, but it is important that the fabric is relatively firm.
CONSTRUCTION	• The magic wand consists of two layers with fiberfill in between. • First crochet two circles. There are two versions of the circles: one with long single crochet stitches and one in a single color. You can choose two of one type or one of each. • The circles are crocheted together and then the six points of the star are worked. • Before finishing the last point, add the embellishments and the bamboo dowel.

- All single crochet stitches are worked as Y-single crochet.
- Each piece is worked in a spiral.

2 X CIRCLES WITH COLOR CHANGES AND LONG SINGLE CROCHET

Color A

Rnd 1: Make a magic ring and work 6 sc around ring (6).

Rnd 2: 6 Iinc (12).

Rnd 3: 6 x [1 sc, 1 Iinc], 1 sc (*to shift beginning of rnd here and for rest of pattern*) (18).

Rnd 4: 6 x [2 sc, 1 Iinc], SCC (24).

Color B

Rnd 5: 6 x [3 sc, 1 Iinc], CR (30).

Rnd 6: 6 x [4 sc, 1 Iinc], SCC (36).

Color C

Rnd 7: 6 x [1 sc, 1 Lsc 2 rnds below (*in the same place where you worked the fourth rnd*), 1 sc, 1 Lsc 1 st to the right and 2 rnds below (*in st straight at of first Lsc*), 1 sc, 1 Iinc], CR (42).

Rnd 8: 6 x [6 sc, 1 Iinc], SCC (48).

Color D

Rnd 9: 2 sc, 1 Lsc 2 rnds below (*in same place as seventh rnd*), 3 sc, 1 Iinc, 5 x [3 sc, 1 Lsc 2 rnds below (*in same place as seventh rnd*), 3 sc, 1 Iinc,], 1 sc (54).

Cut yarn and fasten off.

Make an invisible finishing join and then weave in all ends neatly on WS.

When working long single crochet, if you find that the legs are crossing no matter how you hold your yarn, stop and check before you continue. Adjust the legs so they don't cross on either the front or back of the work.

Now embroider the circle with color E from the center out in every stitch 3 rounds longer as you go out.

Tie the yarn ends together on the wrong side and weave in ends.

Make another circle the same way.

2 X SINGLE-COLOR CIRCLES

You can make an extra single-color star so you'll have a "blank canvas" you can embroider and sew beads onto.

Color A

Rnd 1: Make a magic ring and work 6 sc around ring (6).

Rnd 2: 6 Iinc (12).

Rnd 3: 6 x [1 sc, 1 Iinc], 1 sc (*to shift beginning of rnd here and for rest of pattern*) (18).

Rnd 4: 6 x [2 sc, 1 Iinc] (24).

Rnd 5: 6 x [3 sc, 1 Iinc] (30).

Rnd 6: 6 x [4 sc, 1 Iinc] (36).

Rnd 7: 6 x [5 sc, 1 Iinc] (42).

Rnd 8: 6 x [6 sc, 1 Iinc] (48).

Rnd 9: 6 x [7 sc, 1 Iinc] (54).

Cut yarn and fasten off.

Make another circle the same way.

Embroider or sew beads onto circles.

STAR POINTS, EMBELLISHMENTS, AND MORE

Now you'll make the star points, decorate them, and attach the bamboo dowel. It's important to follow the step-by-step sequence as described below. As needed, check the instructions in the beginning of the book for explanations of the various steps on the following pages.

STEP-BY-STEP SEQUENCE

- Crochet the first four points.
- Sew the first two spaces between the first, second, and third points together.
- Make the decoration you want to hang down from the wand.
- Attach the hanging decoration a little over the hole not sewn together between points 3 and 4.
- Fill the first four points with a bit of fiberfill.
- Crochet the fifth point and sew the space between the fourth and fifth points together.
- Make a little hole in the dowel about 1–1¼ in (2.5–3 cm) down from the top with an awl or something similar.
- Push the dowel into the hole between the third and fourth points (*in the same place as the hanging decoration*).
- Thread a strand of cotton yarn into a tapestry needle, insert it into the hole you made in the dowel, and tie the yarn around securely with a couple of knots.
- Now sew the yarn ends and dowel together securely on the inside of the star. The join should be a little above the hole but not so far up that the end of the dowel goes all the way up against the crochet. The end of the dowel should be a little over the middle so it is covered and ultimately protected by fiberfill.
- Crochet the first couple of rounds of the sixth and last point.
- Fill the star with fiberfill, distributing it smoothly on both sides of the dowel. Add a bit of extra fill at the opening and push it down firmly.
- Finish crocheting the last point and weave in ends.
- Now insert a crochet hook into the last point to ease the fiberfill into the point.

STAR POINTS

The star points are worked over 9 stitches on each of the circles for a total of 18 stitches. Wherever you have long single crochet, count 4 stitches out on each side.

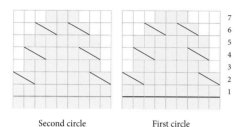

Second circle   First circle

Make a slip knot, making sure there is an end long enough to sew the spaces together later.

Color A

Rnd 1: Make 9 sc in the first circle. Place the second circle so the circles lie with WS facing WS and work 9 sc on the second circle (*you'll once again crochet over 9 sts so they match and the long single crochet at the center*).

Now continue in the round.

Rnd 2: 2 x [1 dec, 5 sc, 1 dec] (14).

Rnd 3: 1 sc in each st around (14).

Rnd 4: 2 x [1 dec, 3 sc, 1 dec] (10).

Rnd 5: 1 sc in each st around (10).

Rnd 6: 2 x [1 dec, 1 sc, 1 dec] (6).

Rnd 7: 1 sc in each st around (6).

Cut yarn and fasten off.

Now sew the point together by using overhand stitch over the back loops of each of the 6 remaining stitches. Tighten well; pull loose end to WS and fasten off.

When crocheting the following points, begin by loosening the slip knot on the opposite side of the yarn end from the previous point. That is, if you began all your points in circle 1, place the next point to the right of the previous one. This way, you can be sure that you have yarn ends for sewing up all the in-between spaces.

SEWING THE SPACES TOGETHER

Thread yarn end on a tapestry needle.

1. Bring needle out from WS in the same place as the last sc you worked on the previous point.

2. Sew straight over and in from RS at corresponding stitch on opposite layer.

3. Now insert needle "diagonally" under on WS so you come out at the same place where you worked the first sc on next point.

4. Sew straight over and in from RS at corresponding stitch on opposite layer.

Tighten yarn well and repeat so you have two strands over each seam.

Pull yarn in to WS and cut yarn.

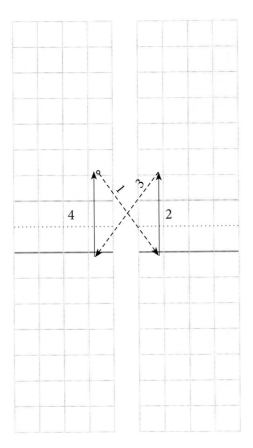

HANGING DECORATION

You can use whatever you'd like to create something sweet for the hanging decoration. Check to see if you have some pretty, thin ribbon in your stash, for example—something glittery, or satin, lacy, or with sequins. You can also make a variety of different custom ribbon effects with yarn as I have done with a crocheted spiral and a braid (see below).

CROCHETED SPIRAL

You'll need a crochet hook in size U.S. C-2 (2.5 mm) and one strand of Shiny.

Ch 60–70, turn with ch 1.

Row 1: Work 2 sc in each st.

If you don't think your spiral is twisted enough, you can work 3 sc in each chain st instead of 2.

Cut yarn and fasten off. Make sure that the loose yarn end is long enough so it can be incorporated as part of the decoration.

BRAID

- Cut three strands of yarn, approx. 15¾ in (40 cm) each.
- Join the strands by knotting them together at the center.
- On one side of the knot, leave the end as is for loose yarn strands in the decoration.
- Braid the three strands on the other side of the knot until they are a suitable length, approx. 6–7 in (15–18 cm).
- Knot the end of the braid to make a tiny tassel; trim tassel even.

FINISHING

- Once you have all the elements for your hanging decoration, tie them together like a tassel. I tied the spiral together with the braid at the knot and added a few loose strands of yarn.
- Take the crochet hook and insert it from the WS out into the space between the third and fourth star points. Grab the hanging decoration and pull it in on the WS so you can sew the decoration securely a little bit above the hole and thereby hide the knots.

BACKPACK

This small backpack with a lace pattern can be worn like a little carryall for food and drinks, gym shoes, a change of clothes, and much more. It can be completely personalized, so I've included quite a few charts for letters and motifs. Write your child's name or initials or choose from a variety of motifs—you can combine different charts in many different ways. If you already have in mind specific motifs that are perfect for your recipient but that aren't included here, all you have to do to design them yourself is draw small x's on graph paper.

SIZES	One size
CROCHET HOOK	U.S. D-3 (3 mm)
YARN	Color A (*base*): 50 g Organic Cotton Color B (*lace*): 75 g Organic Cotton Color C (*embroidery*): small amount of Shiny and/or Organic Cotton
NOTIONS	The number of specific colors you'll need depends on how many motifs and colors your final design will include. • Jacket cords: approx. ⅛ in (3–4 mm) in diameter, approx. 2¼ yd (2 m) long • I recommend using jacket cord because it will slide more easily through the top holes than a crocheted cord.
GAUGE	28 sts x 32 rnds = 4 x 4 in (10 x 10 cm) in X-sc worked in the round. Adjust hook size to obtain correct gauge if necessary.
CONSTRUCTION	• Begin by crocheting the two small strap loops. • Next, make the base and crochet on the two strap loops at the same time. • Embroider the motifs on the base. • Then, crochet the lace section. • Finally, thread the jacket cords through and sew the strap loops to the base.
TIPS	You can adapt the charts for the letters and motifs to make small beaded decorations of all sorts. For example, you can make a lovely row of pennants featuring unicorns with manes in a variety of colors, or a nameplate to put on the door to a child's room.

2 X STRAP LOOPS

Begin by crocheting two strap loops, which will be crocheted securely to each side of the base piece when you assemble the base later.

The straps are crocheted in a rather special way:

- Ch 2.
- Make 1 sc in the first ch; turn the work so you can work 1 sc in the second ch.
- Turn work (*without a turning st*) so you can make 1 sc in the two loops at the side, turning it toward the hook's handle.
- Turn work again (*without a turning st*) and make 1 sc in the two top loops at the side.
- Continue the same way (*from * to * in the drawings below*) until strap loop is desired length.
- Cut yarn and fasten off, making sure to leave a long yarn end for sewing the strap loops together so you can adjust their size once you thread in the jacket cords.

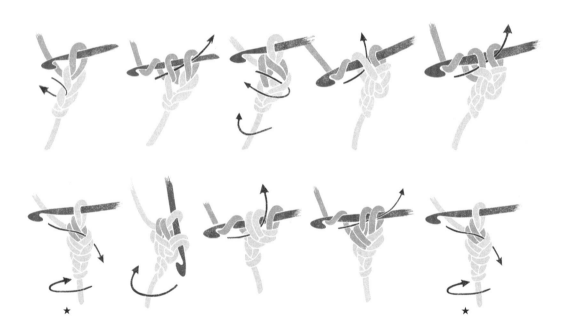

BACKPACK BASE

NOTES

- Work all single crochet as X-single crochet stitches.
- The piece is worked in a spiral.

Color A

Ch 64 + 1 extra ch to turn.

Rnd 1: Work 1 sc in each ch across and then continue around to other side of chain and work 1 sc in each ch (128).

Rnd 2: Work 1 sc in each st around (128).

Rnd 3: Work 1 sc in each st around, except last 2 sts (128).

Now crochet the strap loops securely over the next 4 sts as follows:

Insert hook in on one side of one end of the strap loop, then insert hook into next st and work 1 sc as normal.

Now insert hook in on other side of same end, insert hook in next st and work 1 sc as normal.

Repeat this on the other end of the strap loop over the next 2 sts.

Work 60 sc.

Crochet the other strap loop (*over 4 sts*) on the other side. End with 60 sc. The round now begins 2 sts before the side of the bag—this will be important later on, when you begin the lace section.

Wait before weaving in ends of strap loops, because they will be used later for sewing the strap loops together, in order for the hole in the strap loop to accommodate the thickness of the jacket cord you've chosen.

Rnds 4–19: Work 1 sc in each st around (128).

If you want to embroider the unicorn or dragonfly motif, work another 3 rnds for a total of 22 rnds, because these motifs need a bit more length.

Cut yarn and fasten off.

Make an invisible finishing join and weave in end on WS.

Because the work will roll up a bit, it's a good idea to steam-press it now. That way, you can manipulate the piece a little so the stitches will lie over each other as smoothly as possible. This will ensure that your embroidery will stay smooth and not slanted.

EMBROIDERING NAMES AND MOTIFS

If you want to embroider a name, initials, or anything else on the backpack base, it's best to do so now before you continue to the next section.

NOTES

- The motifs are embroidered using cross stitch.
- You can embroider with one strand either of glitter or cotton yarn (*color C*). Make sure that there is a strong contrast between the motif and the background color.
- The embroidery is worked on one side corresponding to the last stitches of the round. This is primarily in relation to the lace, which will be crocheted later—here, the beginning of the round shifts throughout and will be most visible on the opposite side. Of course, you can also embroider on both sides.

TIPS

- You can include several small details in your embroidery. When embroidering each of the unicorns, for example, I embroidered a few long lines in the mane in a darker tone than the mane itself. On the rainbow clouds, I first embroidered with natural white Organic Cotton and then embroidered again on top with Shiny White, also working the cross stitches opposite those underneath.

PLACEMENT OF EMBROIDERY

Begin by looking over the alphabet and motif charts. Count how many stitches your chosen motif has across its width. If a name is too long to fit, you can embroider a nickname or initials instead and add a sweet motif.

For a starting point, place the letters 3 rounds down from the top and motifs 2 rounds from the top (*if more rounds on the base have been added on purpose, this will create a better balance, so the name and motifs will be more visible when the backpack has items in it*).

Be especially careful when embroidering certain motifs or letters such as Q, since they go over or under the suggested standard number of rounds. You can adjust and fit them all neatly in one or more rounds up or down.

Example

S E L M A: 8 + 8 + 8 + 10 + 8 = 42.

A space of 1 stitch before and after each letter is included, but the extra space can be omitted from the first and last letters: 42 − 2 = 40.

To calculate the total number of extra stitches, subtract the number of stitches for the name or motif from the number of stitches in the width of the base:

64 − 40 = 24.

To determine how many stitches there need to be on each side of the complete name or motif, divide the extra stitches by two: 24 / 2 = 12.

So, you'll count 12 stitches in at each side, and the name or motif begins 3 rounds from the top.

EXAMPLE

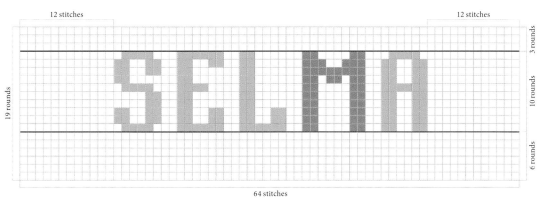

LACE

NOTES

- Work all single crochet as X-single crochet stitches.
- The first round begins where you ended the base; e.g., 2 stitches before the side of the bag (*left side, when looking at the embroidery*). When working the lace, make sure that the 8 lace holes at each side of the backpack lie symmetrically over each other.

Change to color B.

Rnd 1: *4 sc, ch 4, skip the next 4 sts* (128).

Rnd 2: *4 sc, 6 sc around ch lp,* work 5 sl sts (*to shift beginning of rnd here and for rest of pattern*) (160).

Rnd 3: *4 sc in the center 4 of the 6 sc of previous rnd, ch 4, skip next 6 sts* (128).

Rnd 4: *4 sc, 6 sc around ch lp,* 5 sl sts (160).

Repeat Rnds 3–4 until you've worked a total of 18 rnds of lace holes, but on the last rnd (*with lace*) where you would crochet around ch lp (*corresponding to the fourth rnd*), instead work as follows:

Last Rnd: *4 sc, 4 sc around ch lp* (128).

Do not cut yarn but continue around on the top.

Rnds 1–3: Work 1 sc in each st around (128).

On the next rnd, make the holes for the jacket cord.

Because the beginning of the round is now shifted a little to the front, begin by working 62 sc so you are on the opposite side—the new beginning of round.

Rnd 4: 6 sc, 8 x [ch 3, skip next 3 sts, 4 sc], 8 sc, 8 x [ch 3, skip next 3 sts, 4 sc], 2 sc (128).

Rnd 5: Work 1 sc in each st around, with 3 sc around each ch lp (128).

Rnds 6–7: Work 1 sc in each st around (128).

Rnd 8: Work 1 sl st in each st around (128).

Cut yarn and fasten off.

Make an invisible finishing join and weave in ends neatly on WS (*except for the ends of the straps*).

JACKET CORDS

Insert the two jacket cords (*they should measure about 39½ in [1 meter] each*).

Lay the backpack flat and work as follows:

Insert cord up through the lowest strap loop at right side.

Now push cord down through first hole on right side and up through next hole to the left before the first hole.

Continue, weaving cord in and out until all the way around; end by coming up from the last hole of the round.

Insert the cord down through the strap loop and make a knot with the two ends.

Repeat the sequence in reverse on the left side.

To prevent the cords from coming out of the strap loops, you can sew the strap loops together a bit in order to make the hole a little smaller. Use the loose ends from the strap loop and stitch from the bag and out to the knot until you see that the hole is the right size.

CHART

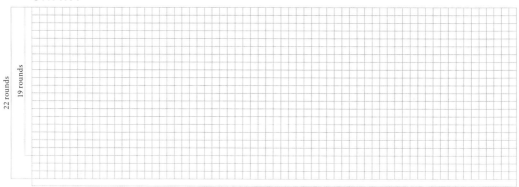

22 rounds
19 rounds

64 stitches

ALPHABET

6 stitches across

8 stitches across

9 stitches across

10 stitches across

When placing letters, these blocks should be on the line.

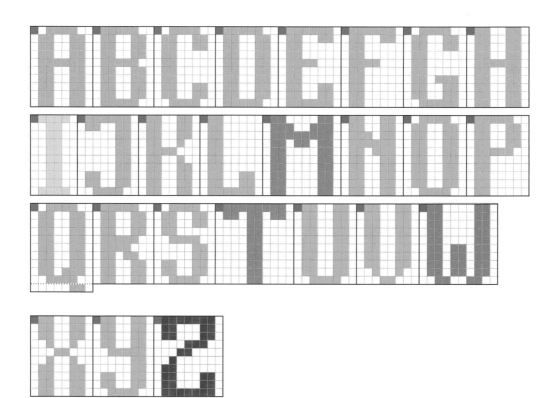

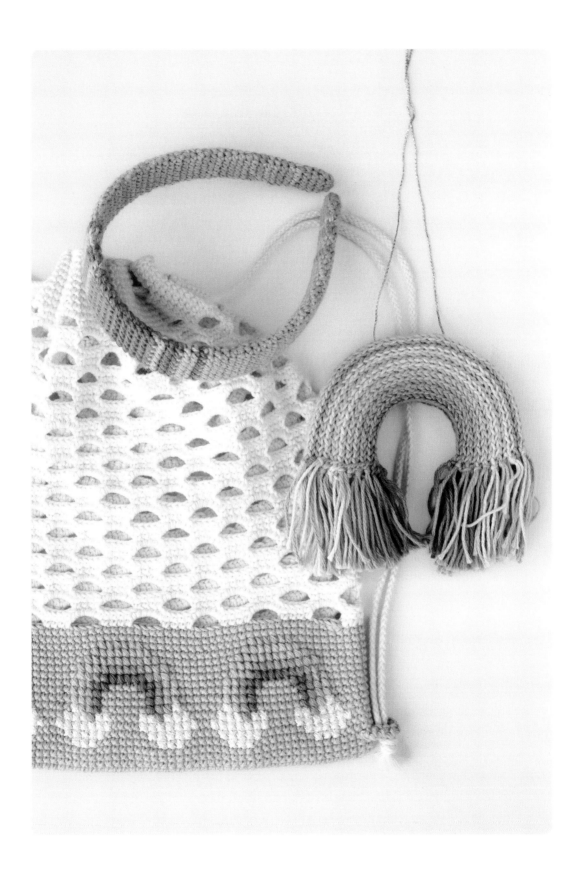

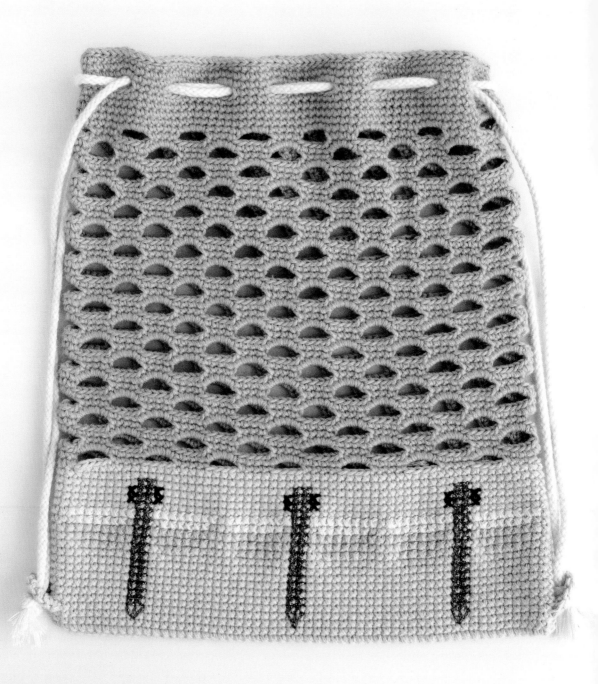

BACKPACK CHARTS

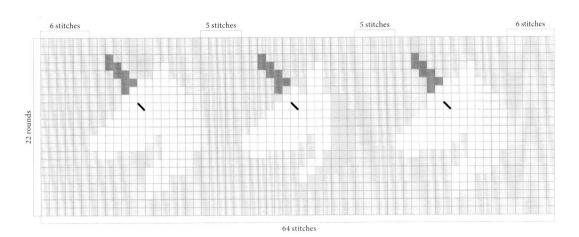

6 stitches   5 stitches   5 stitches   6 stitches

22 rounds

64 stitches

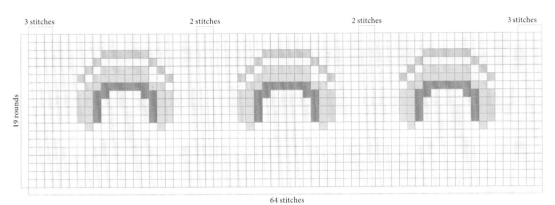

3 stitches   2 stitches   2 stitches   3 stitches

19 rounds

64 stitches

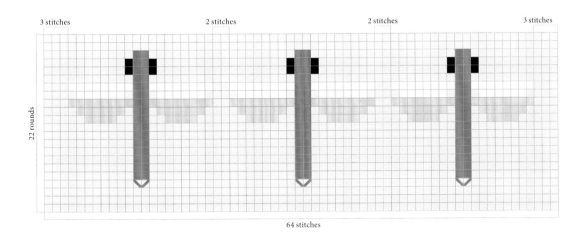

3 stitches   2 stitches   2 stitches   3 stitches

22 rounds

64 stitches

UNICORN WALL HANGING

You'll work with several small balls of yarn of the same color for this detailed picture. Don't worry, though—the directions specify whenever you need to use the different balls. If you haven't previously tried multicolor crochet, this is a good project to start with. The eye and mouth are embroidered on afterward. The mane, made with mixed shades of leftover yarns, creates a 3-D effect as it cascades over the frame.

CROCHET HOOK	U.S. D-3 (3 mm)
YARN	Color A (*background*): 50 g Organic Cotton Color B (*head*): 15 g Organic Cotton Color C (*horn*): small amount of Shiny Color D (*eye and mouth*): small amount of Shiny Mane—use one or more colors as you prefer: Colors E1–E4: small amount of Organic Cotton Color E5: Shiny
NOTIONS	• Two bamboo dowels or something similar, approx. ¼ in (7–8 mm) in diameter, approx. 8¼–9 in (21–23 cm) long
GAUGE	24 sts x 30 rows = 4 x 4 in (10 x 10 cm) in Y-sc worked back and forth. Adjust hook size to obtain correct gauge if necessary.
CONSTRUCTION	• Begin by crocheting a flat canvas that includes the head and horn, crocheted back and forth in rows. • Next, embroider the eye and mouth. • Crochet the accent lines and hanging cord. • Attach lengths of yarn for the mane and trim mane.

"CANVAS" BACKGROUND

NOTES

- Work all single crochet as Y-single crochet stitches.
- Turn all rows with ch 1.

Color A

Ch 51 + 1 extra ch for turning.

Row 1 (WS): Work 1 sc in each ch across (51).

Row 2 (RS): Work 1 sc in each st across (51).

Rows 3–9: Work 1 sc in each st across (51).

Row 10: Work 1 sc in each st across, but, on this row, crochet the piece together to create a casing for the bottom dowel.

Fold the piece lengthwise and begin by inserting hook under both stitch loops on the first layer (*as you normally would*), then insert hook into back loop of the first ch on row and finish as for 1 sc. Continue the same way across (51).

Rows 11–18: Work 1 sc in each st across (51).

Now begin making the unicorn's head. Make sure you are careful when changing colors.

NOTES

- ⇒ means that you should change colors. All the color changes are made with a sharp color change—that is, you should finish the stitch before the color change (the last stitch of the original color) by bringing the new color through on the last step of that stitch.
- To avoid carrying colors A and B back and forth between the different sections, crochet from several small balls of the same color— wind up a little yarn so you have two extra small balls of color A and one extra small ball of color B.
- Begin by crocheting from the two different balls of color A (*A1 and A2*) and 1 ball of color B.
- When you start to crochet the muzzle, work from three balls of color A (*A1, A2, and A3*) and two balls of color B (*B1 and B2*).

Row 19: 24 sc ⇒ B, 2 sc ⇒ A2, 25 sc.

Row 20: 23 sc ⇒ B, 3 sc ⇒ A1, 25 sc.

Row 21: 25 sc ⇒ B, 5 sc ⇒ A2, 21 sc.

Row 22: 19 sc ⇒ B, 6 sc ⇒ A1, 26 sc.

Row 23: 27 sc ⇒ B, 6 sc ⇒ A2, 18 sc.

Row 24: 17 sc ⇒ B, 6 sc ⇒ A1, 28 sc.

Row 25: 29 sc ⇒ B, 6 sc ⇒ A2, 16 sc.

Row 26: 15 sc ⇒ B, 6 sc ⇒ A1, 30 sc.

Row 27: 9 sc ⇒ B2, 5 sc ⇒ A3, 17 sc ⇒ B1, 6 sc ⇒ A2, 14 sc.

Row 28: 13 sc ⇒ B1, 7 sc ⇒ A3, 16 sc ⇒ B2, 7 sc ⇒ A1, 8 sc.

Row 29: 7 sc ⇒ B2, 9 sc ⇒ A3, 16 sc ⇒ B1, 7 sc ⇒ A2, 12 sc.

Row 30: 11 sc ⇒ B1, 8 sc ⇒ A3, 15 sc ⇒ B2, 11 sc ⇒ A1, 6 sc.

"CANVAS" BACKGROUND CHART

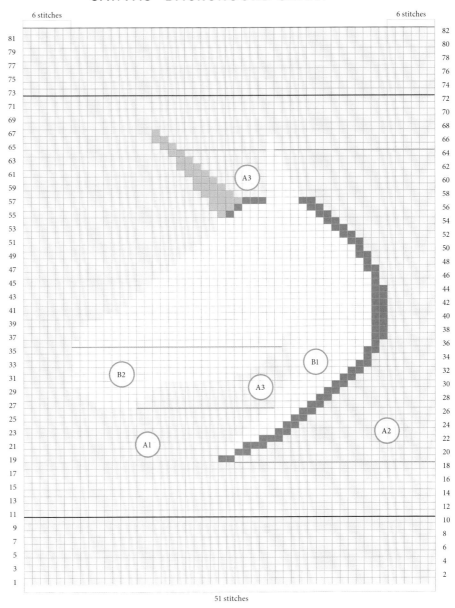

6 stitches

6 stitches

82 80 78 76 74 72 70 68 66 64 62 60 58 56 54 52 50 48 46 44 42 40 38 36 34 32 30 28 26 24 22 20 18 16 14 12 10 8 6 4 2

81 79 77 75 73 71 69 67 65 63 61 59 57 55 53 51 49 47 45 43 41 39 37 35 33 31 29 27 25 23 21 19 17 15 13 11 9 7 5 3 1

A3 B1 B2 A3 A1 A2

51 stitches

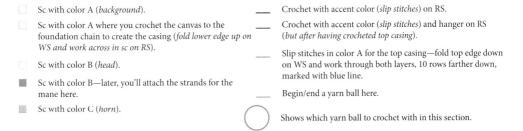

☐   Sc with color A (*background*).

☐   Sc with color A where you crochet the canvas to the foundation chain to create the casing (*fold lower edge up on WS and work across in sc on RS*).

☐   Sc with color B (*head*).

■   Sc with color B—later, you'll attach the strands for the mane here.

▨   Sc with color C (*horn*).

—   Crochet with accent color (*slip stitches*) on RS.

—   Crochet with accent color (*slip stitches*) and hanger on RS (*but after having crocheted top casing*).

—   Slip stitches in color A for the top casing—fold top edge down on WS and work through both layers, 10 rows farther down, marked with blue line.

—   Begin/end a yarn ball here.

◯   Shows which yarn ball to crochet with in this section.

Row 31: 6 sc → B2, 20 sc (*crochet around color A3*) → A3, 7 sc → B1, 8 sc → A2, 10 sc.

Row 32: 9 sc → B1, 9 sc → A3, 5 sc → B2, 22 sc → A1, 6 sc.

Row 33: 6 sc → B2, 23 sc → A3, 4 sc → B1, 10 sc → A2, 8 sc.

Row 34: 8 sc → B1, 10 sc → A3, 3 sc → B2, 24 sc → A1, 6 sc.

Row 35: 6 sc → B2, 25 sc → A3 (*end B2*), 2 sc → B1, 11 sc → A2, 7 sc.

Row 36: 7 sc → B1, 11 sc → A3, 1 sc → B1, 26 sc → A1, 6 sc.

Row 37: 7 sc → B, 25 sc → A3, 1 sc → B (*end A3 for now*), 12 sc → A2, 6 sc.

Row 38: 6 sc → B, 38 sc → A1, 7 sc.

Row 39: 8 sc → B, 37 sc → A2, 6 sc.

Row 40: 6 sc → B, 35 sc → A1, 10 sc.

Row 41: 12 sc → B, 33 sc → A2, 6 sc.

Row 42: 6 sc → B, 32 sc → A1, 13 sc.

Row 43: 14 sc → B, 31 sc → A2, 6 sc.

Row 44: 6 sc → B, 30 sc → A1, 15 sc.

Row 45: 16 sc → B, 28 sc → A2, 7 sc.

Row 46: 7 sc → B, 27 sc → A1, 17 sc.

Row 47: 18 sc → B, 26 sc → A2, 7 sc.

Row 48: 8 sc → B, 24 sc → A1, 19 sc.

Row 49: 20 sc → B, 23 sc → A2, 8 sc.

Row 50: 9 sc → B, 21 sc → A1, 21 sc.

Row 51: 22 sc → B, 20 sc → A2, 9 sc.

Row 52: 10 sc → B, 18 sc → A1, 23 sc.

Row 53: 24 sc → B, 16 sc → A2, 11 sc.

Row 54: 12 sc → B, 15 sc → A1, 24 sc.

Row 55: 24 sc → C, 1 sc → B, 13 sc → A2, 13 sc.

Row 56: 14 sc → B, 11 sc → C, 3 sc → A1, 23 sc.

Row 57: 23 sc → C, 4 sc → B, 9 sc → A2, 15 sc.

Row 58: 17 sc → B, 4 sc → A3, 4 sc → C, 4 sc → A1, 22 sc.

Row 59: 21 sc → C, 4 sc → A3, 5 sc → B, 4 sc → A2, 17 sc.

Row 60: 18 sc → B, 3 sc → A3, 6 sc → C, 3 sc → A1, 21 sc.

Row 61: 20 sc → C, 3 sc → A3, 7 sc → B, 3 sc → A2, 18 sc.

Row 62: 19 sc → B, 2 sc → A3, 8 sc → C, 3 sc → A1, 19 sc.

Row 63: 19 sc → C, 2 sc → A3, 9 sc → B, 2 sc → A2, 19 sc.

Row 64: 20 sc → B (*end A2*), 1 sc → A3, 10 sc → C (*end A3*) 2 sc → A1, 18 sc.

Row 65: 17 sc → C, 2 sc → A, 11 sc → B, 1 sc → A, 20 sc.

Row 66: 20 sc → B, 1 sc → A, 12 sc → C, 2 sc → A, 16 sc.

Row 67: 16 sc → C, 1 sc → A, 34 sc.

Rows 68–82: 1 sc in each st across.

After crocheting last row, turn and cut yarn.

Ch 1, turn and fold top edge down. Now make the top casing. Make a row of slip stitches on WS—first insert hook under both stitch loops of last sc you worked. Then insert hook 10 rows down (*marked with a blue line on chart*), yarn over hook, and bring yarn through both layers and loop on hook. Continue the same way across row.

Cut yarn, fasten off, and weave in all ends neatly on WS.

EMBROIDERY

Embroider the eye and mouth with one strand of black Shiny. Cut yarn and weave in ends.

EDGINGS AND HANGER

I recommend making the edgings and hanger now, before beginning the mane. It is much easier to trim the mane evenly when you are ready to hang the panel.

Crochet a row of slip stitches (*with RS facing*) in the same place where you joined the casing (*marked with the blue line on the chart*). There should be 5 rows between the slip stitch line and the tip of the unicorn horn.

Once you've worked all the way across, continue with ch 60–70; cut yarn and fasten off.

Join the two loose ends and weave in ends.

Crochet a row of slip stitches on lower edge of hanging (*with RS facing*) over the casing (*marked with the red line on the chart*). The slip stitches should be placed so there are 8 rows from that line to the beginning of the unicorn.

FINISHING

Gently steam-press the hanging under a damp pressing cloth—this makes a big difference and flattens and smooths the stitches.

Insert a dowel in each casing.

Finish with the hanger, wrapping it once around on each side of the dowel so the hanger comes up from the back of the panel. This way, the panel will hang flush against the wall when hung up.

MANE

COLORS AND LENGTH

Cut a number of strands in a variety of colors to use for the mane. I used four colors.

Throughout, I paired two colors together, so I had three different color combinations for a pretty color progression. I used about three different lengths. Some were relatively short, for the forehead locks. Some were half-length, for the lower part of the mane and body. The full-length strands were for the top and sides of the mane.

Method for attaching the strands:

- Take two strands and fold them at the middle.
- Insert the crochet hook into a stitch (*read more about how to do this in "Suggestions for Attaching Strands" at right*), grip the middle of the strands and bring them through so you make a loop with the two strands.
- Grab the four loose ends and bring them through the loop without pulling the ends.
- Tighten the loop first, then tighten the loose ends.

SUGGESTIONS FOR ATTACHING STRANDS

This section really digs into the nitty-gritty, but it is okay if you don't proceed exactly as described. I just want to explain to you how I worked and the logic behind my method.

You can insert the crochet hook in from all four sides as well as across the stitches. You can attach more or fewer strands in service of the look you want to achieve. When attaching strands, you can choose the direction you want the strands to come out in. The direction you insert the hook in from is the direction the strands will turn.

- For the forehead locks, I decided to insert the hook in from the left side of the stitch so that the strands would turn toward the left.
- At the top and side of the mane, I inserted the hook in from the right so that the strands would turn toward the right.
- For the lower part of the mane and body, I inserted the hook in from the left so that the strands would turn toward the left.
- Finally, I added highlights with single strands of Shiny placed at the top.
- For these thin highlights, I inserted the hook in from the top so the strands would stay and lay nicely on top.

TRIMMING THE MANE

Finish the hanging by trimming the mane, just cutting it roughly at first.

Hang the panel and then do a final trim to neaten everything nicely.

HAIR SCRUNCHIE

Decorative hair scrunchies are great for embellishing ponytails and buns—
and they also work nicely as small armbands. Dig into your yarn stash
to use up some of your scraps.

SIZES	One size
CROCHET HOOK	U.S. D-3 (3 mm)
YARN	Color A1: small amount (4–6 g) Organic Cotton Color B1: small amount (2–3 g) Shiny or Organic Cotton You can add an extra main color (A2) as well as an extra edging color (B2) if you want—in which case, you'll need fewer grams of each color.
NOTIONS	• Elastic scrunchie band (metal-free)—I used a band about 6¾ in (17 cm) in circumference.
GAUGE	Gauge is not important here, but you do need to be sure you don't crochet too loosely or tightly.
CONSTRUCTION	• The scrunchie is crocheted around the elastic band. • The edging is worked on both right and wrong sides.
TIPS	When you look at the different scrunchies, it looks as if they were crocheted differently, but they were actually made in exactly the same way. They used the same kind of yarn, the same size of elastic band, the same number of stitches, the same type of stitches, and the same number of rounds. The only difference is the color and how many times the edge is "folded" while finishing. Whenever there is too much material at the edge in relation to the circumference of the band, folds will naturally occur as shown, creating the ruffles all around the scrunchie. You can manipulate the edge and decide how many times the ruffle should go up and down. The more times you "fold" the edge, the smaller the ruffles will be (*as in the dusty-rose scrunchie*), and, conversely, the ruffles will be bigger if you "fold" the edge fewer times (*as in the white scrunchie*).

NOTE

- Work all single crochet as Y-single crochet stitches.

Color A1

Begin working sc around the elastic band as follows:

Rnd 1:

- Make a slip knot.
- Insert hook in under band, catch yarn and bring yarn through so you have two loops on hook. With hook over band, catch yarn and pull yarn through both loops.
- Make as many sc around band as needed to cover it—and crochet around the starting end so you won't have to weave it in later. Make more sts than you think are needed—I worked a total of 80 sc, but the number depends on your band. Make sure to push the sts tightly together—you do not need to go up to a specific number.
- When you've worked all the way around, end with 1 sl st into first sc of rnd (*bring color A2 through if you are using two main colors*).

Rnd 2:

- Ch 2, work 2 dc in each st—begin in the sl st you ended with.
- After working all the way around, end with 1 sl st into second ch.
- Cut yarn but do not fasten off—leave loop on hook.
- Insert hook under both st loops of next st and bring color B1 through.

- **Rnd 3:**

- 1 sl st (*under both st loops*) in each st around.
- Cut yarn and fasten off.
- Make an invisible finishing join and weave in ends.

Rnd 4:

- Make a slip knot with color B1 (*or B2, if you have two different edge colors*), remove hook from loop and leave loop to rest.
- Take band and turn it so you can crochet on the opposite side of previous round with sl sts.
- Insert hook into same place as previous round of sl sts (*the hook comes out under the sl sts on the opposite side*).
- Place resting loop back on hook and bring loop through.
- Work 1 rnd with 1 sl st in each st—work in same places as for sl sts on opposite side. Make sure throughout that the hook comes out under the opposite sl st on the other side.
- Cut yarn and fasten off.
- Make an invisible finishing join and weave in ends.

Now adjust the edge on the band so the folds are pretty. You can "fold" the edge many times for small and tight ruffles, as in the dusty-rose scrunchie, or fewer times so the ruffles look higher, as in the pale gray scrunchie.

PENNANT BANNER

Make a lovely garland to sparkle up a child's room. If the individual pennants are made with casings, you can rearrange them to display any message the day calls for!

You can also make a special birthday garland, perhaps with a child's name and birthdate, or with a simple "Happy Birthday" so it can be used for the whole family.

SIZES	One size A single pennant measures 4¼ in (11 cm) in width and 5¼ in (13.5 cm) in length.
CROCHET HOOK	U.S. D-3 (3 mm)
YARN	Color A (*main color*): 25 g Organic Cotton Color B (*motif*): 25 g Organic Cotton or Shiny Color B (*accent lines*): small amount Organic Cotton or Shiny
NOTIONS	• Jacket cord, approx. ⅛ in (3–4 mm) diameter The length for the cord depends on how many pennants you will be hanging on it; each pennant measures approx. 4¼ in (11 cm) across. If you want to make a hanging knot at each end, you'll need approx. 23¾ in (60 cm) of additional length. For a garland with five pennants and hanging knots, I used a total of approx. 51 in (130 cm) of cord.
GAUGE	Gauge is not important here, but you do need to be sure you don't crochet too loosely or tightly.
CONSTRUCTION	• Begin by crocheting the background and motif, worked back and forth. • Next, add the accent lines. • String the pennants onto the cord, then make the optional hanging knots at each end.

PENNANT

NOTES

- Work all single crochet as Y-single crochet stitches.
- Turn all rows with ch 1.
- All bobbles are worked on the WS.
- All color changes are made with a sharp color change—that is, you should finish the stitch before the color change (the last stitch of the original color) by bringing the new color through on the last step of that stitch.
- When crocheting rows on RS, be aware of color changes, and also be aware whether or not you need to bring along color B for a couple of stitches (*you'll do this by simply crocheting around the strands of color B*), so that color B is already there and ready to be worked for the next row of bobbles.
- When you work with the bobble color, always work around color A (*crocheting around the strands of color A*).
- There is no chart for the number "0." Use the chart for the letter "O."

Color A

Ch 12 + 1 extra ch to turn.

Row 1 (WS): 1 sc in each ch (12).

Row 2 (RS): 2 inc, 8 sc, 2 inc (16).

Row 3: 1 inc, 14 sc, 1 inc (18).

Row 4: 1 inc, 16 sc, 1 inc (20).

Row 5: 1 inc, 18 sc, 1 inc (22).

Row 6: 1 sc in each st (22).

If the motif is a Q, it begins on the next row; read Notes before you continue crocheting.

Row 7: 1 inc, 20 sc, 1 inc (24).

Row 8: 1 sc in each st (24).

All motifs other than Q begin on the next row; read Notes before you continue crocheting.

Row 9: 1 sc in each st (24).

Row 10: 1 inc, 22 sc, 1 inc (26).

Rows 11–40: 1 sc in each st (26).

Do not cut yarn; continue to edge.

EXAMPLE

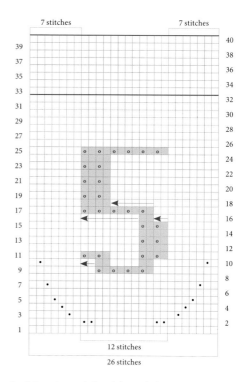

Read chart alternately from left to right (*on WS, odd-numbered rows*) and from right to left (*on RS, even-numbered rows*).

☐ No stitch

☐ Sc with color A

▪ 2 sc in same stitch (inc) with color A

▫ Bobble with color B

▪ Sc with color B

◄┐ Crochet around this color while is not in use.

___ Join casing edges here.

EDGING

Ch 1 and, with RS facing, work in sc down along edge and all the way around the curve (*at the ch 12, skip the first and last sts for a neater curve*) and up to the opposite corner. Work approx. 1 st per row/st and make sure you crochet relatively firmly.

Do not cut yarn; leave it hanging for casing.

CASING

When you reach the right corner, make the loop a bit longer, remove hook from loop, and let it rest (*do not work a row on top*). Cut yarn and fasten off, making sure to leave a yarn end about 31½ in (80 cm) long to be used for joining the casing (*if you want to be sure you leave enough yarn, loosely ch 26. Add 4–6 in [10–15 cm] of yarn, cut yarn, and unravel chain sts*).

With RS facing, count 8 rows down (*marked with red line on chart*), insert hook under both st loops of sc worked at edge, catch loose yarn end, and bring it through to RS (*hold finger on the resting loop so you don't pull it out*).

Place hook back into resting loop and tighten loop a bit. Fold the casing on top with WS facing WS so you can join the two layers with a row of slip sts (*with WS facing*) as follows:

Insert hook under both loops (on first sc of row), then insert hook into back layer (*8 rows down*), yarn over hook, and bring through both layers and loop on hook. Continue the same way across the row until you come to the place where you made a sc at the edge. Now insert hook under both stitch loops of edge st on back layer, yarn over hook, and bring loose yarn end all the way on last step.

Weave in ends.

ACCENT LINES

Make a slip knot, remove hook from loop, and let it rest. Insert hook (*from RS*) into left corner at the place where the casing was joined meets the place where you worked the edge st. Catch resting loop and bring it through to RS. Work sl sts all the way around and up to opposite corner. Continue with sl st in same row as you joined casing—make last sl st in same place where you brought loop up from WS.

Cut yarn and fasten off. Make an invisible finishing join and weave in ends.

FINISHING

- Gently steam press under a damp pressing cloth—this makes a big difference in helping the stitches and embroidery lie smooth and flat.

- When you've made all the pennants, you can string them onto your jacket cord.

HANGING KNOTS

You can make a looped hanging knot at each end of the cord so you can hang the garland easily. I chose to make knots like these because I think they add a nice finish. The technique isn't difficult, but here are a couple of suggestions to help.

Make the hanging knots as follows:

1. Fold the cord once about 9¾ in (25 cm) from the end, so the end pokes up. Then fold the cord once by about 2 in (5 cm), so the end points down.

2. Make sure you have an "eye" free below the first fold. Now wrap the end of the cord around all three cords about 7–8 times until only a little eye is left.

3. Finish by sticking the end of the cord through the eye as shown and tighten the knot. Trim the end.

4. Now you can adjust the size of the loop as needed.

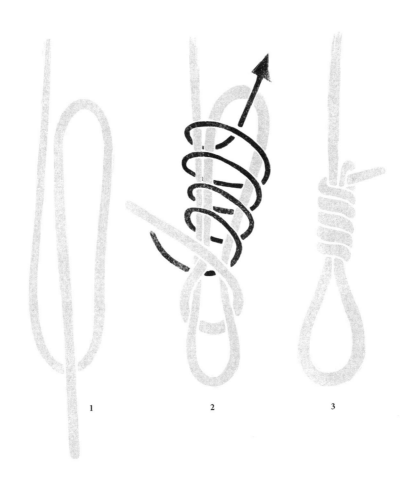

1   2   3

A B C D

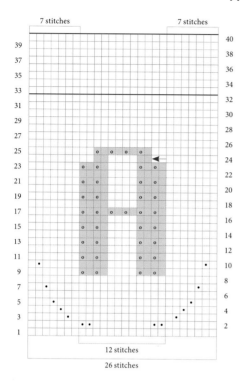

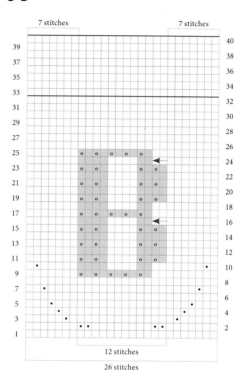

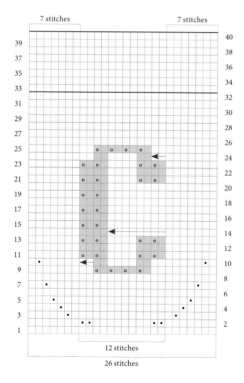

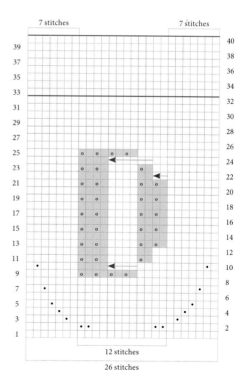

E F G H

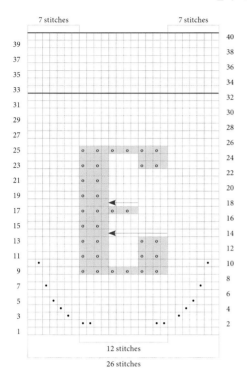

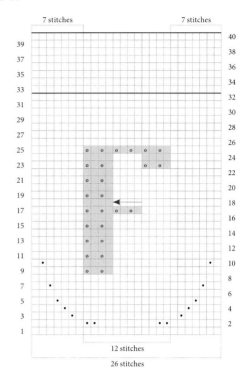

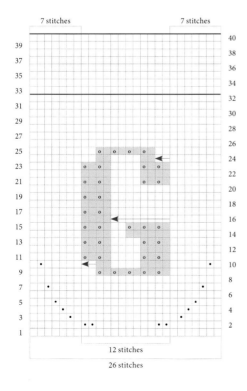

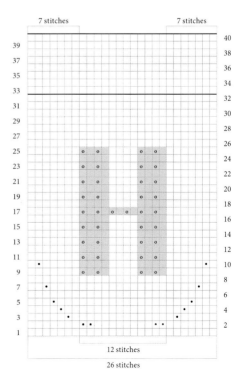

I J K L

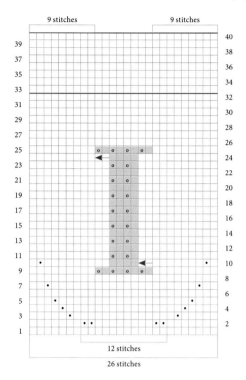

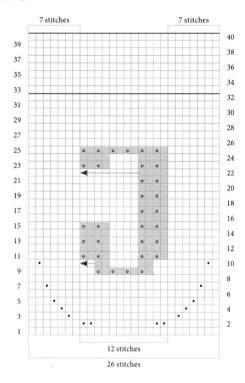

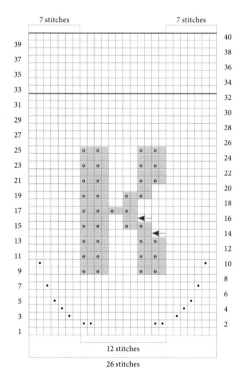

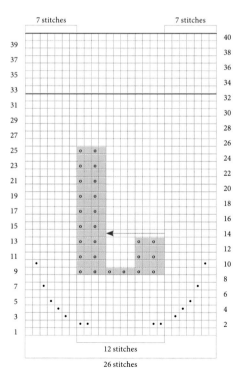

M N O P

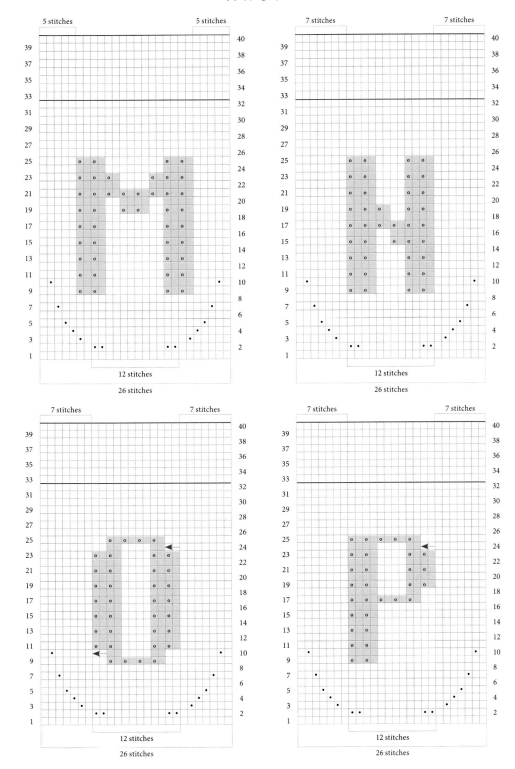

QRST

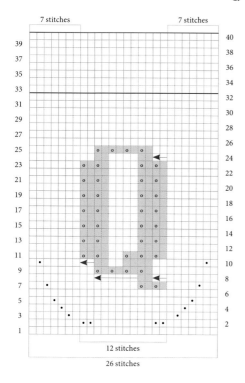

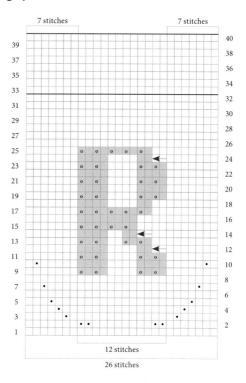

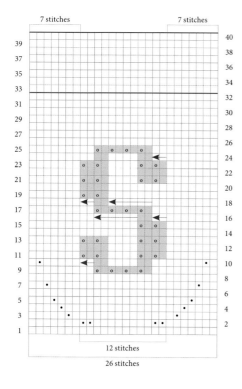

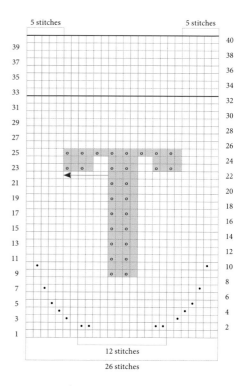

U V W X

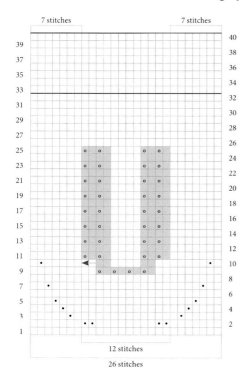

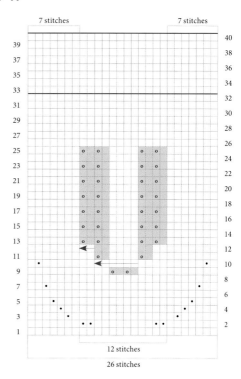

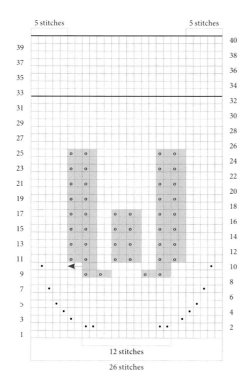

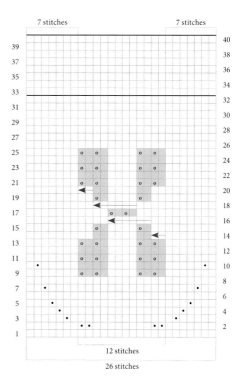

Y Z

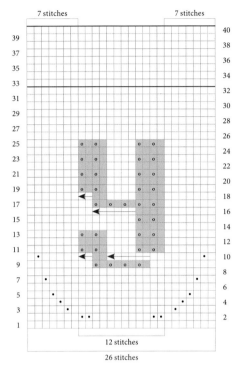

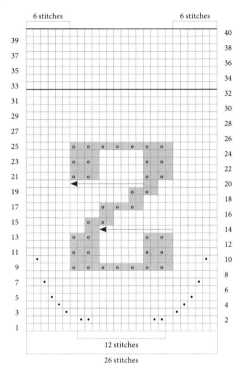

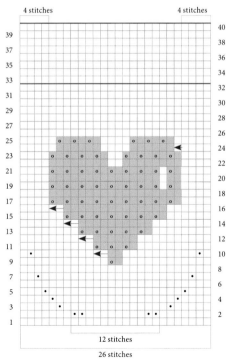

1 2 3 4

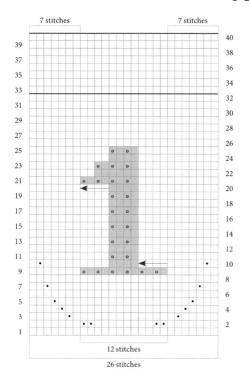

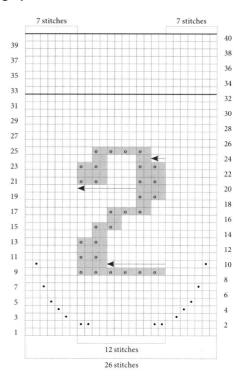

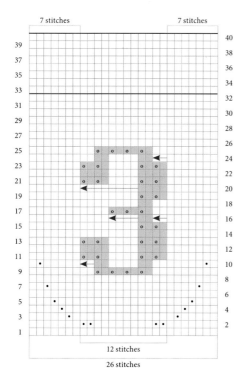

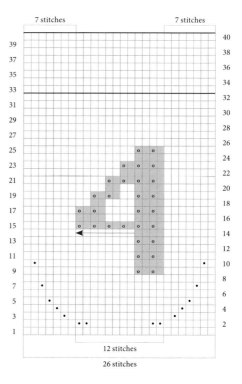

5 6 7 8

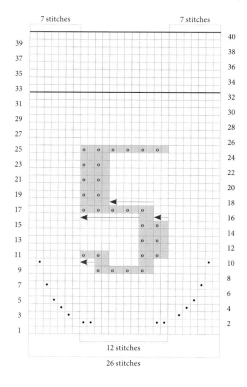

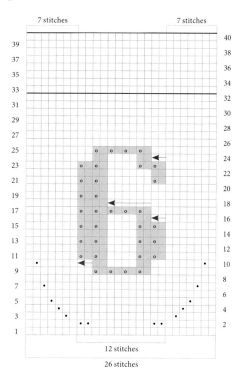

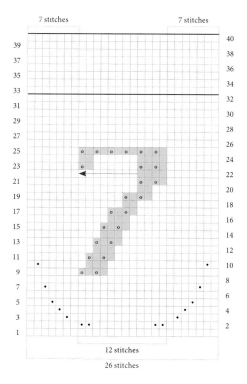

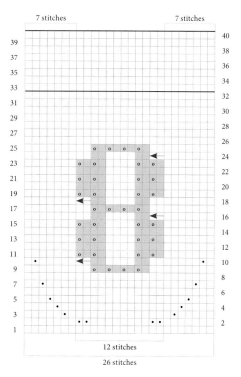

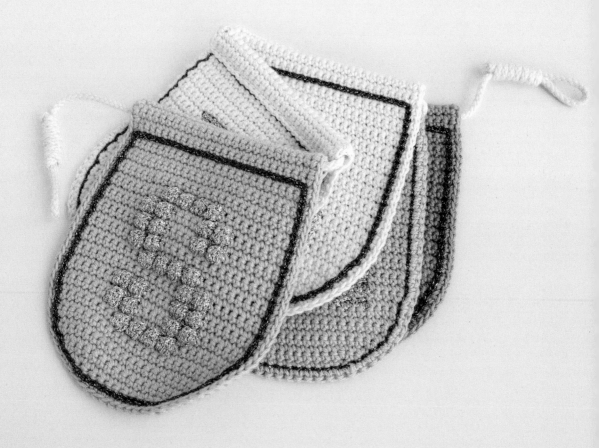

9

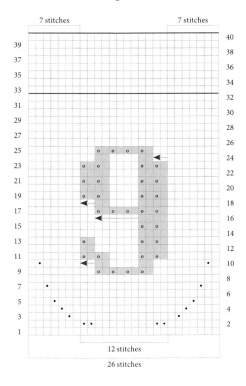

		7 stitches						7 stitches			

39
37
35
33
31
29
27
25
23
21
19
17
15
13
11
9
7
5
3
1

40
38
36
34
32
30
28
26
24
22
20
18
16
14
12
10
8
6
4
2

12 stitches

26 stitches

PLAY CROWN

This is truly your opportunity to get creative and play. The pattern provided gives you a basic form with two different heights to choose from, and you can also choose the colors, stripes, embroidery, and embellishments. You can sew a symphony of beads in all colors of the rainbow, or embroider on a delicate grooved edging of wildflowers or a little butterfly. Your imagination is the only limit. The design of the ribbon tie allows the crown to fit heads of all sizes, and, once it's sewn on, you don't need to adjust it every time.

SIZES	Information is provided for two sizes: short (tall in parentheses) The crown measures approx. 15¾ in (40 cm) wide and approx. 3 (3½) in (7.5 [9] cm) high (excluding ribbon tie).
CROCHET HOOK	U.S. C-2 (2.5 mm)
YARN	Color A (*main color*): 50 (75) g Organic Cotton Color B (*edging*): small amount (4–5 g) Shiny Optional: several colors for embroidery. The high crown might require an extra 50 g of yarn.
NOTIONS	• Ribbon tie, approx. ⅝–1 in (15–25 mm) wide, 39½–45¼ in (100–115 cm) long • Stiff iron-on interlining (Vlieseline H 250), approx. 15¾ in (40 cm) x 3 (3½) in (7.5 [9] cm) • Beads, buttons, and other items for embellishment (optional)
GAUGE	28 sts x 34 rows = 4 x 4 in (10 x 10 cm) worked back and forth in Y-sc. Adjust hook size to obtain correct gauge if necessary.

The construction of this crown has been thought through carefully. The crown is, of course, meant for play, but it's also important that it is comfortable to wear. Therefore, it's made in two layers, and the inner layer, which lies directly against the head, is completely free of anything that could irritate the wearer. The back side of any embellishments, embroidery, beads, etc., is all covered. The interlining is ironed on so you can be sure that the crown will hold its shape and not droop or become misshapen due to the weight of beads or other decorations.

CONSTRUCTION

The sequence of steps for constructing the crown is important. When I mention "front" and "back," this indicates the right and left sides of the charts (*not the right and wrong sides of the pieces*).

The embroidery is done, for example, on the front—that is, the right side of the chart.

Then, when the crown is folded, it folds so that wrong side faces wrong side.

CONSTRUCTION SEQUENCE

(Refer to page 97 to see visual illustrations showing the following construction sequence.)

- The crown is crocheted in rows with decreases and increases. It is completed with a round of single crochet all the way around the piece on the right side.
- Accent lines of slip stitches are worked on the right side of the front of the crown.
- Next, the crown is embellished with embroidery and/or beads sewn onto the front.
- Then, a ribbon tie is sewn onto the wrong side of the front in against the centerline / fold line.
- A piece of stiffening interlining is ironed onto the wrong side of the front.
- Finally, the crown is folded at its center with wrong side facing wrong side and crocheted together with slip stitches on the right side.

TIPS

If the ribbon tie you've chosen is pretty and an important detail for you, you can make it a bit longer so that it hangs from the bow down the back of the wearer's neck. For example, the tie plays an important aesthetic role in the striped variation that's otherwise quite subdued. On the white and light-blue variations, the embroidery and beads play the main role.

If you'd prefer, instead of using a ribbon tie, you could sew the crown together with a piece of wide elastic at the back.

To calculate the length of the elastic, do the following:

- Measure the child's head circumference and subtract about ¾ in (a couple of centimeters).
- Now subtract the length of the crown from that measurement.
- Add a sufficient seam allowance to that number. This is how long your piece of elastic should be.
- Now sew each end of the elastic securely to each end of the crown (*on wrong side*).
- Follow the remaining instructions from this point on.

NOTES

- Work all single crochet as Y-single crochet stitches.
- Turn all rows with ch 1.
- Make all decreases and increases as regular decreases and increases.
- Remember that the instructions include the stitch numbers for the tall size crown in (parentheses) directly after the stitch numbers for the short size crown, or in [brackets] instead of parentheses when the number is indicating the total stitch count at the end of a row.

The pattern for the crown is written out here, but you can follow the charts on pages 94–95 instead if you prefer—just note that the finishing edging is not included on the chart.

Color A

Ch 22 (30) + an extra ch 1 for turning.

Row 1 (WS): 1 sc in each ch (22 [30]).

Row 2 (RS): 1 inc, 1 sc in each st until 1 st rem, 1 inc (24 [32]).

Row 3: 1 sc in each st (24 [32]).

Repeat Rows 2–3 until you've worked the increase row a total of 5 times (including Row 2) and have a total of 32 (40) sts across.

Row 12: 1 dec, sc in each st until 2 sts rem, 1 dec (30 [38]).

Row 13: 1 sc in each st (30 [38]).

Repeat Rows 12–13 until you've worked the decrease row a total of 5 times (including Row 12) and have a total of 22 (30) sts across.

Row 22: 1 inc, 1 sc in each st until 1 st rem, 1 inc (24 [32]).

Row 23: 1 sc in each st (24 [32]).

Repeat Rows 22–23 until you've worked the increase row a total of 7 times (including Row 22) and have a total of 36 (44) sts across.

Row 36: 1 dec, sc in each st until 2 sts rem, 1 dec (34 [42]).

Row 37: 1 sc in each st (34 [42]).

Repeat Rows 36–37 until you've worked the decrease row a total of 7 times (including Row 36) and have a total of 22 (30) sts across.

Row 50: 1 inc, 1 sc in each st until 1 st rem, 1 inc (24 [32]).

Row 51: 1 sc in each st (24 [32]).

Repeat Rows 50–51 until you've worked the increase row a total of 9 times (including Row 50) and have a total of 40 (48) sts across.

Row 68: 1 dec, sc in each st until 2 sts rem, 1 dec (38 [46]).

Row 69: 1 sc in each st (38 [46]).

Repeat Rows 68–69 until you've worked the decrease row a total of 9 times (including Row 68) and have a total of 22 (30) sts across.

Row 86: 1 inc, 1 sc in each st until 1 st rem, 1 inc (24 [32]).

Row 87: 1 sc in each st (24 [32]).

Repeat Rows 86–87 until you've worked the increase row a total of 7 times (including Row 86) and have a total of 36 (44) sts across.

Row 100: 1 dec, sc in each st until 2 sts rem, 1 dec (34 [42]).

Row 101: 1 sc in each st (34 [42]).

Repeat Rows 100–101 until you've worked the decrease row a total of 7 times (including Row 100) and have a total of 22 (30) sts across.

Row 114: 1 inc, 1 sc in each st until 1 st rem, 1 inc (24 [32]).

Row 115: 1 sc in each st (24 [32]).

Repeat Rows 114–115 until you've worked the increase row a total of 5 times (including Row 114) and have a total of 32 (40) sts across.

Row 124: 1 dec, sc in each st until 2 sts rem, 1 dec (30 [38]).

Row 125: 1 sc in each st (30 [38]).

Repeat Rows 124–125 until you've worked the decrease row a total of 5 times (including Row 124) and have a total of 22 (30) sts across—omit the last row with 1 sc in each st.

Do not cut yarn; instead proceed directly to edging.

EDGING

Continue, crocheting up and along the edge and all the way around the piece. Work 1 sc in each st/row, working 2 sts into the top of each point (= Rows 11, 35, 67, 99, and 123). Also work 2 sts into the four corners if you want them to be more pointed.

Cut yarn and fasten off.

Make an invisible finishing join and weave in ends neatly on WS.

Before going any further, gently steam-press the crown under a damp pressing cloth so it will lie nice and flat.

ACCENT LINES

Now crochet the accent lines.

- The accent lines are created in a contrast color (*Shiny, for example*) and worked in slip stitches on the RS.
- Begin at top and work down along the rows of center stitches on right side; this is also marked on the chart above the embroidery.
- Continue working in sl st along the edge, in the same place where you worked the final single-crochet edge.
- Continue until you've gone all the way around.
- Cut yarn and fasten off.
- Make an invisible finishing join and weave in ends neatly on WS.

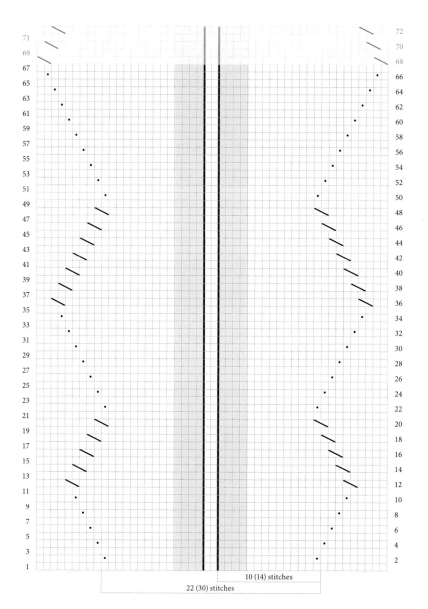

10 (14) stitches

22 (30) stitches

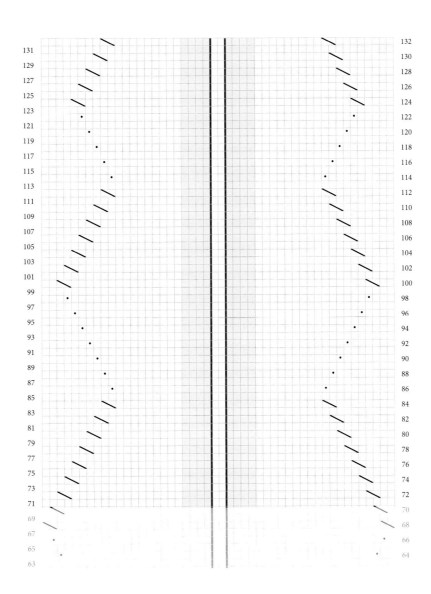

EMBROIDERY AND BEAD ACCENTS

You're finally at the "play" phase—it's time to add embroidery and sew on beads. All the embroidery is done on the RS of the crown, within the framing of the accent lines.

Don't forget that the WS will be hidden when the crown is folded, so you don't need to be an expert at embroidery—don't worry about how the back looks.

On the following pages, I describe how I decided to decorate my crowns, but these are, of course, only ideas to inspire your own creativity.

Once you've decorated the crown and before you go any further, give the crown another gentle ironing / steam pressing so it will lie smoothly (*iron on wrong side and make sure none of the beads melt!*).

RIBBON TIE

The ribbon tie is sewn on the WS of the right (front) side—in toward the centerline / fold line. It should not be farther in toward the center than the accent line.

Fold the ribbon tie to determine its center and lay it on the crocheted piece so the center of the tie aligns with the center of the crown. Use sewing thread to sew the band securely with overhand stitch. I sewed all the way around the band to make the stitching extra strong and to distribute the tension evenly over a larger area (when the tie is ultimately knotted tightly).

You could also choose to sew two short, separate ribbon ties securely on each side of the WS, instead of one single long one as described above.

If your chosen ribbon tie is a material or weave that may unravel at the ends, fold each end over a couple of times and sew it down.

INTERLINING

Lay a piece of stiff interlining over the crown (front side) and trace around it so it fits neatly inside the accent lines.

Cut the interlining. Place the glue side down on the WS of the front side of the crown (*where the accent lines, embroidery, and band all are*). Iron on the interlining (*without using steam*) by holding the iron over the whole piece for approx. 5–8 seconds.

FINISHING

With WS facing WS, fold crown along center line.

Make a slip knot with color A.

Remove hook from loop and let it rest.

Insert hook in from RS under both stitch loops on edge st (*sc*), directly over the tie band on the right side (*below in relation to the chart, or what corresponds to the left side when wearing it*).

Place resting loop back on hook and draw it through on last stitch step.

Now continue crocheting, working 1 sl st in each sc on the edge all the way around until you come to the tie band on the opposite side.

Cut yarn and fasten off.

Take yarn to WS and weave in end.

Construction summary:

1. Crochet an accent line of slip stitches on RS of front.

2. Decorate the crown with embroidery and/or sew beads on front.

3. Sew ribbon tie on WS of front in toward centerline / fold line.

4. Iron on a piece of stiff interlining on WS of front.

5. Finally, fold crown at middle with WS facing WS, and crochet together with sl sts on RS.

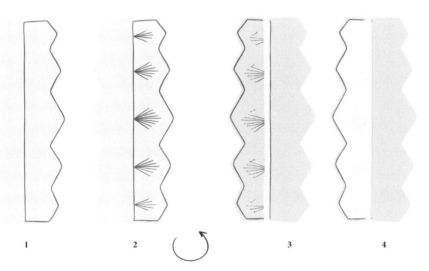

Flip over to WS.

STRIPED CROWN
(SHORT)

For the striped variation, I finished crocheting with one row of slip stiches on RS in all the spaces at color changes—that is, crocheting over the surface along every other row. Be careful to follow all these extra rows if you want the crown to be a bit wider. Afterward, you can steam press the opposite piece and manipulate it a little so it is somewhat larger.

There will be many yarn ends to weave in if you crochet all the slip stitch rows from the same direction, since you will have to cut the yarn after every slip stitch row.

A little tip is to work two rows with the same strand—that way, you'll eliminate half of the ends you would have otherwise needed to weave in. Begin by working with the loose end (which should be a little long) and crochet the row at the side of the working yarn.

Cut yarn and fasten off.

Wind the ends together on WS and weave them in.

WHITE CROWN WITH BEADS
(TALL)

I made a chart (see page 104) showing how I embroidered a fan pattern with a bead ending each line; note that the chart shows only the right side.

When embroidering over many stitches, as I have done here, be careful about how tightly you tighten the threads, adjusting them as you work so they won't be too loose or too tight.

Ironing on the interlining later will also help secure the threads.

I recommend sewing on beads afterward.

EMBROIDERY FOR WHITE CROWN WITH BEADS

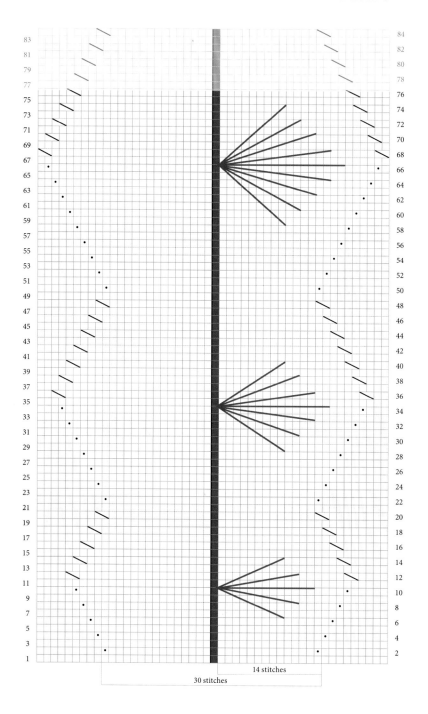

LIGHT-BLUE CROWN
WITH DRAGONFLY
(TALL)

For this version, I began by embroidering a pattern with a lot of silver thread.

When embroidering over many stitches, as I have done here, be careful about how firmly you tighten the threads. Adjust them as you work so they won't be too loose or too tight.

Ironing on the interlining later will also help secure the threads.

On the two outermost sections, at each side, I sewed on three beads.

Next, I made the dragonfly in the center. I began by sewing on beads to make the body and a large faceted crystal half-shank button to make the head. Then I embroidered the legs with a strand of Shiny Copper.

Finally, I crocheted four wings with Shiny White and crochet hook size U.S. C-2 (2.5 mm), then sewed them on.

2 X RIGHT WINGS

Ch 9 + ch 1 to turn.

Rnd 1: 2 sc, 2 hdc, 2 dc, 2 hdc, 4 dc in last ch, ch 1 and continue down along opposite side of foundation chain. Begin with 1 sc around last dc and then work 9 sc.

Cut yarn and fasten off.

2 X LEFT WINGS

Ch 10 + ch 1 to turn.

Rnd 1: 10 sc, ch 1, and continue down along opposite side of foundation chain. Skip the first ch (*where you worked the last sc*), work 4 dc in next st, 2 hdc, 2 dc, 2 hdc, 2 sc.

Cut yarn and fasten off.

Place wings alongside bead body and sew them down securely along middle of foundation chain. Weave in ends.

TEALIGHT LANTERN

With this pattern, you can upgrade your empty jam jars into portable lanterns or nightlights for a child's room or secret hideout. You can add a handle if you want to hang the lights. Or, if lanterns aren't your thing, why not turn these into special holders for your child's collection of markers, colored pencils, and more!

This pattern is unbelievably easy to follow, so an endless number of stitches and rows are not written out. You can make variations to suit any size of jar. You can also use different types of yarn or even work with two strands held together—just make sure that your hook is well matched to your yarn size so you will have a relatively firm structure in the finished piece.

CROCHET HOOK	U.S. D-3 (3 mm)
YARN	Color A (*base*): 25 g Organic Cotton
	Color B (*lace*): 25 g Organic Cotton
	The quantity of yarn you'll need will depend on the size of your glass
NOTIONS	container, but in most cases the amounts shown here will be sufficient.
	• Empty, clean jam jar
	• Optional: LED tealight or LED string lights
GAUGE	Gauge is not important here, but it is important to crochet relatively firmly.
CONSTRUCTION	• Crochet the base first.
	• Crochet the lace next, and finish with the handle.
TIPS	Here are specific measurements for the Weck jars I used; you can compare your jars to these dimensions to come up with your own best size:

Weck 580 ml, 4½ in (11.3 cm) high and 4¼ in (10.8 cm) circumference
Base: 10 sts between increases = 72 sts per round and 5 rounds without decreases.
Lace: about 9 lace holes.

Weck 290 ml, 3½ in (8.75 cm) high and 3½ in (8.8 cm) circumference
Base: 7 sts between increases = 54 sts per round and 4 rounds without decreases.
Lace: about 8 lace holes.

BASE

Work all single crochet as Y-single crochet stitches.

This piece is worked in a spiral.

Color A

Make a magic ring and work 6 sc around ring (6).

Rnd 1: 6 Iinc (12).

Rnd 2: 6 x [1 sc, 1 Iinc] (18).

Rnd 3: 6 x [2 sc, 1 Iinc], 1 sc (*to shift beginning of rnd here and for rest of rnds*) (24).

Rnd 4: 6 x [3 sc, 1 Iinc], 1 sc (30).

Rnd 5: 6 x [4 sc, 1 Iinc], 1 sc (36).

Continue the same way, increasing 6 sts per rnd, until the base is the desired size. I recommend that you crochet 1 round less than you actually calculate you need for the diameter of the jar before you begin working straight up into the lace pattern. The crocheted piece might "grow" a little, and it will look nicest if the sides are crocheted relatively snugly for the jar.

Now work 1 sc in each st—work the number of rounds you think seem best (will fit your jar the nicest) before you start working the lace.

LACE

TIPS

You can work in stripes over 2 rounds. Make color changes by bringing in the new color on the last step of stitch, when working the last of the 4 slip stitches to shift beginning of round.

Color B

Rnd 1: *3 sc, ch 3, skip next 3 sts.*

Rnd 2: *3 sc, 5 sc around ch lp,* 4 sl sts (*to shift beginning of rnd here and for rest of pattern*).

Rnd 3: *3 sc in center of the 5 sc of previous rnd, ch 3, skip next 5 sts.*

Rnd 4: *3 sc, 5 sc around ch lp,* 4 sl sts.

Repeat Rnds 3–4 to desired height, but, on last rnd, where you would work around ch lp (*on Rnd 4*), work as follows instead:

Last Lace Rnd: *3 sc, 3 sc around ch lp.*

Do not cut yarn; decide now if you want to crochet a top without a handle or a top with a handle. Follow the appropriate instructions on the following page.

TOP WITHOUT A HANDLE

- Work 2–3 rnds with 1 sc in each st.
- End with 1 rnd with 1 sl st in each st.
- Cut yarn and fasten off.
- Make an invisible finishing join and weave in ends on WS.

TOP WITH A HANDLE

- Work 2–3 rnds with 1 sc in each st.
- Chain the number of sts for desired handle length (*if you are in doubt, make a relatively long handle—you can always knot the chain to reduce it to the correct length*).
- Join chain to opposite side with 1 sc.
- Work 1 rnd with 1 sl st in each st.
- When all the way around, continue, crocheting over the handle chain with 1 sl st through back loop of each ch.
- Cut yarn and fasten off.
- Make an invisible finishing join and weave in ends on WS.

TASSEL

Add a cute extra detail by attaching a tassel to the bottom of the lantern.

1. Wrap yarn many times around a piece of cardstock or something similar to desired thickness.

2. Tie around the strands with a double half hitch; you can use this tie for finishing.

3. Remove bundle from cardstock and cut bottoms of strands.

4. A little down from the top, tie a strand around the tassel to make the head of the tassel. You can simply wrap a strand around the tassels a couple of times, make a knot, and thread the ends into the tassel. For an even nicer finish, you can finish by "whipping," shown in the drawings below.

5. Trim tassel to desired length and sew tassel to base.

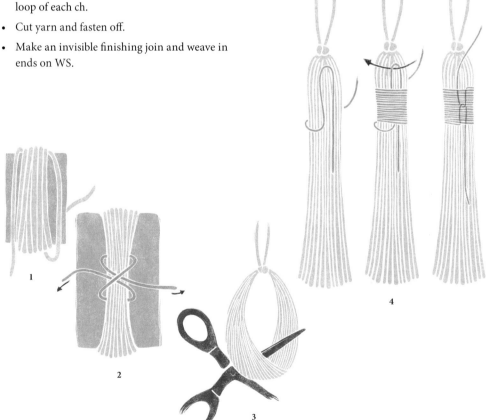

RAINBOW HANGING

Here's a sweet little rainbow hanging you can crochet with just leftover yarns. Or, if you prefer, make a whole set of them in different colorways!

SIZES	Information is provided for two sizes: small (large in parentheses) The small size has five stripes/colors; the large has ten stripes/colors.
CROCHET HOOK	U.S. D-3 (3 mm)
YARN	Color S1 (*stripe 1*): small amount Organic Cotton or Shiny Color S2 (*stripe 2*): small amount Organic Cotton or Shiny Color S3 (*stripe 3*): small amount Organic Cotton or Shiny Color S4 (*stripe 4*): small amount Organic Cotton or Shiny Color S5 (*stripe 5*): small amount Organic Cotton or Shiny
	For the large hanging, use an additional five colors.
	Color H (*hanging cord*): small amount Organic Cotton or Shiny
NOTIONS	• Small length of wire (optional)
GAUGE	Gauge is not important here, but it is important to crochet relatively firmly.
CONSTRUCTION	• Each stripe is worked individually, starting from the innermost stripe, and crocheted back and forth in rows. • The stripes are then sewn together one after another from the center outward. • You can reinforce the hanging with optional wire. • Add fringe and trim it. • Attach a small hanging cord.

NOTES

- Work all single crochet as Y-single crochet stitches.
- Turn all rows with ch 1.
- Make sure you begin and end each stripe (*except for stripe 1*) with a long yarn end; these ends will be used to sew the stripes together.
- Remember that the instructions include the stitch numbers for the large rainbow in (parentheses) directly after the stitch numbers for the small rainbow, or in [brackets] instead of parentheses when the number is indicating the total stitch count at the end of a row.

STRIPE 1

Ch 24 (30) + ch 1 extra for turning.

Row 1: 1 sc in each ch in the little loop behind ch st (24 [30]).

Rows 2–4: 1 sc in each st (24 [30]).

Cut yarn, fasten off, and move on to next stripe.

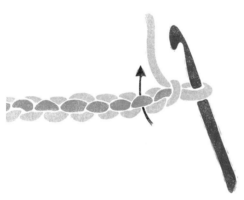

STRIPE 2

Ch 26 (32) + ch 1 extra for turning.

Row 1: 1 sc in each ch in the little loop behind ch st (26 [32]).

Rows 2–4: 1 sc in each st (26 [32]).

Cut yarn, fasten off, and move on to next stripe.

STRIPE 3

Ch 28 (34) + ch 1 extra for turning.

Row 1: 1 sc in each ch in the little loop behind ch st (28 [34]).

Rows 2–4: 1 sc in each st (28 [34]).

Cut yarn, fasten off, and move on to next stripe.

STRIPE 4

Ch 30 (36) + ch 1 extra for turning.

Row 1: 1 sc in each ch in the little loop behind ch st (30 [36]).

Rows 2–4: 1 sc in each st (30 [36]).

Cut yarn, fasten off, and move on to next stripe.

STRIPE 5

Ch 32 (38) + ch 1 extra for turning.

Row 1: 1 sc in each ch in the little loop behind ch st (32 [38]).

Rows 2–4: 1 sc in each st (32 [38]).

Cut yarn and fasten off.

If you want to crochet the larger rainbow, make another 5 stripes. For each stripe, increase the foundation chain by 2 sts.

JOINING THE STRIPES

I decided to join my stripes with a seam that would not be completely invisible so that the colors fade into each other.

Place stripe 1 over stripe 2; they should face the same way so both beginning ends are on the same side.

With the yarn ends from stripe 2 (*each at their own corner*), sew both ends together as follows:

- The stitch loops on each side of a row form small Vs. Each V consists of a loop on top and a loop on bottom. When you sew them together, always stitch through these two loops.

- With the yarn end from stripe 2, begin by sewing into the first st of stripe 1, coming out from the first st of stripe 2.

- Now sew in the second st of stripe 2 and come out from the second st on stripe 1.

Continue the same way across the row, noting that there are two places on the shortest stripe where you will sew into the same stitch two times.

Stripes with 24, 26, 28 sts:

Stitch two times into st #5 at beginning/end of row.

Stripes with 30, 32, 34, 38 sts:

Stitch two times into st #7 at beginning/end of row.

Stripes with 40, 42, 44, 48 sts:

Stitch two times into st #9 at beginning/end of row.

Once you've joined the first two stripes together on both sides, continue to the next stripe. Throughout, sew with the loose ends from the uppermost stripe.

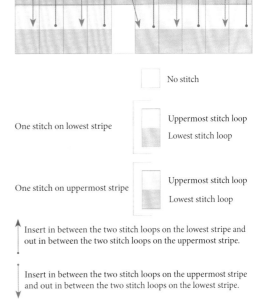

No stitch

One stitch on lowest stripe — Uppermost stitch loop / Lowest stitch loop

One stitch on uppermost stripe — Uppermost stitch loop / Lowest stitch loop

↑ Insert in between the two stitch loops on the lowest stripe and out in between the two stitch loops on the uppermost stripe.

↓ Insert in between the two stitch loops on the uppermost stripe and out in between the two stitch loops on the lowest stripe.

WIRE

Inserting wire is not necessary, but it can help you adjust the final shape of the rainbow and hold it in place.

- Cut a long length of wire and double it up several times—I first made a circle that I then pressed "flat." Make the finished wire a little shorter than the middle stripes of the rainbow. If desired, wrap a little bit of tape around the wire ends so they don't catch the yarn.
- Push the wire in between the two layers of two of the middle stripes.
- Adjust the shape to make your final rainbow.

FRINGE

Add strands for fringe the end of each stripe in the same color as the stripe. Use five strands at each end of each stripe.

Make the fringe as follows:

- Cut a length of yarn about 4 in (10 cm) long in the same color as stripe.
- Fold strand at center.
- With RS facing, insert hook into edge and then out at end of stripe.
- Catch yarn and bring it through, making a loop.
- Yarn around the two loose yarn ends and draw them through the loop.
- Tighten the loop first and then the two ends.
- After attaching all the fringe, trim each to approx. 1–1¼ in (2.5–3 cm).

HANGING CORD

Finally, attach a little length of yarn for hanging the rainbow.

- Cut a piece of yarn (*I used Shiny*) about 13¾ in (35 cm) long.
- Insert yarn under the 8 center sts at middle of top stripe.
- Knot ends and bring knot through to WS.

SUN HAT

This sun hat has glitter yarn detailing crocheted around the top to catch the sun's rays, but it won't bother your child's face. It's an elegant summer hat to fit almost anyone!

As an alternative to the small embroidered feathers, you can make the top yellow like the sun and embroider rays of sunlight down along the sides of the hat. The top could also sport a happy face. Let your imagination loose on this design!

SIZES	Information is provided for three sizes: small (medium, large). The corresponding head circumferences are approx. 18½–19¼ (19¾–21¼, 21¾+) in (or 47–49 [50–54, 55+] cm). If your gauge is correct, the circumference will measure 19 (20⅞, 22½) in (or 48 [52.8, 57.6] cm).
	Head circumference can vary widely within a single age group, so I recommend using the measurement of the circumference. But the sizes listed roughly correspond to 1–3 years for the small, 3–7 years for the medium, and 7+ years for the large.
	Once you've crocheted the top and measured its diameter, you can decide if you need to go up or down a size so the hat will fit properly.
CROCHET HOOK	U.S. D-3 (3 mm)
YARN	Color A (*top*): 25 g Shiny Color B (*body and brim*): 50 (50, 75) g Organic Cotton
GAUGE	25 sts x 29 rows = 4 x 4 in (10 x 10 cm) in Y-sc crocheted in the round. Adjust hook size to obtain correct gauge if needed.
CONSTRUCTION	• The hat is crocheted from the top down. • It is finished with feather motifs embroidered on at the end.

TOP

NOTES

- Work all single crochet as Y-single crochet stitches.
- The hat is crocheted around in a spiral.
- Remember that the instructions include the stitch numbers for the medium and large hat sizes in (parentheses) directly after the stitch numbers for the small hat size, or in [brackets] instead of parentheses when the number is indicating the total stitch count at the end of a row.

Color A

Rnd 1: Make a magic ring and work 6 sc around ring (6).

Rnd 2: 6 Iinc (12).

Rnd 3: 6 x [1 sc, 1 Iinc], 1 sc (*to shift beginning of rnd here and for rest of pattern*) (18).

Rnd 4: 6 x [2 sc, 1 Iinc], 1 sc (24).

Rnd 5: 6 x [3 sc, 1 Iinc], 1 sc (30).

Rnd 6: 6 x [4 sc, 1 Iinc], 1 sc (36).

Rnd 7: 6 x [5 sc, 1 Iinc], 1 sc (42).

Rnd 8: 6 x [6 sc, 1 Iinc], 1 sc (48).

Rnd 9: 6 x [7 sc, 1 Iinc], 1 sc (54).

Rnd 10: 6 x [8 sc, 1 Iinc], 1 sc (60).

Rnd 11: 6 x [9 sc, 1 Iinc], 1 sc (66).

Rnd 12: 6 x [10 sc, 1 Iinc], 1 sc (72).

Rnd 13: 6 x [11 sc, 1 Iinc], 1 sc (78).

Rnd 14: 6 x [12 sc, 1 Iinc], 1 sc (84).

Rnd 15: 6 x [13 sc, 1 Iinc], 1 sc (90).

Rnd 16: 6 x [14 sc, 1 Iinc], 1 sc (96).

Rnd 17: 6 x [15 sc, 1 Iinc], 1 sc (102).

Rnd 18: 6 x [16 sc, 1 Iinc], 1 sc (108).

Rnd 19: 6 x [17 sc, 1 Iinc], 1 sc (114).

Rnd 20: 6 x [18 sc, 1 Iinc], 1 sc (120).

If you are making the small hat, skip directly to Rnd 25.

Rnd 21: 6 x [19 sc, 1 Iinc], 1 sc (126).

Rnd 22: 6 x [20 sc, 1 Iinc], 1 sc (132).

If you are making the medium hat, skip directly to Rnd 25.

Rnd 23: 6 x [21 sc, 1 Iinc], 1 sc (138).

Rnd 24: 6 x [22 sc, 1 Iinc], 1 sc (144).

Rnd 25: 1 sc in each st around (120 [132, 144]).

After Rnd 25, the diameter of the top should be approx. 5¾ (6¼, 6⅞) in (or 14.5 [16, 17.5] cm).

Change to color B (*using the color change for stripes method*), but wait to cut the color A yarn.

Rnd 26: 1 sc in each st around (120 [132, 144]).

Before continuing, work 1 rnd of sl sts in color A in exactly the same place as you crocheted the first rnd of color B. By finishing this way, you'll make a very neat and sharp color change between colors A and B.

Work as follows:

- Insert hook in under both stitch loops of first st on rnd, catch yarn, and bring it though to RS with a loop.
- Continue working sl st around.
- Cut yarn and fasten off.
- Now make an invisible finishing join and weave in ends on WS.

BODY

Continue, working 1 sc in each st around until you've worked a total of 20 (22, 24) rnds with color B or until the body measures 2¾ (3, 3¼) in (or 7 [7.5, 8.5] cm). Of course, you can make the body longer or shorter, as you prefer.

Do not cut yarn; instead continue directly to brim.

BRIM

Rnd 1: 12 x [9 (10, 11) sc, 1 Iinc] (132 [144, 156]).

Rnd 2: 1 sc in each st around (132 [144, 156]).

Rnd 3: 5 (5, 6) sc, 11 x [1 Iinc, 10 (11, 12) sc], 1 Iinc, 5 (6, 6) sc (144 [156, 168]).

Rnd 4: 1 sc in each st around (144 [156, 168]).

Rnd 5: 12 x [11 (12, 13) sc, 1 Iinc] (156 [168, 180]).

Rnd 6: 1 sc in each st around (156 [168, 180]).

Rnd 7: 6 (6, 7) sc, 11 x [1 Iinc, 12 (13, 14) sc], 1 Iinc, 6 (7, 7) sc (168 [180, 192]).

Rnd 8: 1 sc in each st around (168 [180, 192]).

Rnd 9: 12 x [13 (14, 15) sc, 1 Iinc] (180 [192, 204]).

Rnd 10: 1 sc in each st around (180 [192, 204]).

If you are making the small size, skip directly to Rnd 15 for a normal-size brim. If you want a wider brim, continue with Rnd 11.

Rnd 11: 7 (7, 8) sc, 11 x [1 Iinc, 14 (15, 16) sc], 1 Iinc, 7 (8, 8) sc (192 [204, 216]).

Rnd 12: 1 sc in each st around (192 [204, 216]).

If you are making the medium size, skip directly to Rnd 15 for a normal-size brim. If you want a wider brim, continue with Rnd 13.

Rnd 13: 7 (8, 8) sc, 11 x [1 Iinc, 15 (16, 17) sc], 1 Iinc, 8 (8, 9) sc (204 [216, 228]).

Rnd 14: 1 sc in each st around (204 [216, 228]).

Rnd 15: 1 rnd of crab sts.

Rnd 16: 1 sl st in each st (*these are worked in the same place where you crocheted crab sts = one rnd farther down, above the surface along Rnd 14*).

Cut yarn and fasten off.

Make an invisible finishing join and weave in ends on WS.

EMBROIDERY

Finish the hat by embroidering 12 small "feathers" along the edge of the top of the hat using one strand of color A. There should be 8 (10, 12) sts between each feather.

See chart below for the embroidery motif. Because the hat was worked with Y-sc, the rounds will shift and the feathers will be on the diagonal.

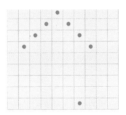

Embroider from the lowest point/stitch of the "ear" to each of the other points/stitches.

RAINBOW TAPESTRY

This is such an enjoyably tactile piece for a child's room. First you crochet a simple panel with a casing along with 3D bobbles for clouds. Finally, you embroider the rainbow in cross stitch. Cross stitches are a great companion to crochet. By working the colors of the rainbow in cross stitch rather than crocheting them as part of the panel itself, you'll avoid having to make tons of color changes and dealing with tangled yarn.

CROCHET HOOK | U.S. D-3 (3 mm)

YARN | Color A (*background*): 50 g Organic Cotton
Color B (*clouds*): small amount (5–7 g) Shiny

For the rainbow, approx. 1–2 g per color:
Color C: Organic Cotton or Shiny
Color D: Organic Cotton or Shiny
Color E: Organic Cotton or Shiny
Color F: Organic Cotton or Shiny
Color G: Organic Cotton or Shiny

NOTIONS | • Two bamboo dowels or similar, ¼ in (7–8 mm) diameter, 8¼–9 in (21–23 cm) long

GAUGE | 24 sts x 30 rows = 4 x 4 in (10 x 10 cm) in Y-sc crocheted back and forth.
Adjust hook size to obtain correct gauge if needed.

CONSTRUCTION | • Begin by making the panel with clouds, crocheted back and forth in rows.
• Embroider the rainbow with cross stitch.
• Finish with accent lines and the hanging cord.

PANEL

NOTES

- Work all single crochet as Y-single crochet stitches.
- Turn all rows with ch 1.

Color A

Ch 48 + ch 1 extra for turning.

Row 1 (WS): 1 sc in each ch (48).

Row 2 (RS): 1 sc in each st (48).

Rows 3–9: 1 sc in each st (48).

Row 10: 1 sc in each st, but, on this row, you'll join the end for a casing on the bottom edge:

Fold the panel down to foundation chain. Insert hook under both stitch loops of first layer (*as normal*), then insert hook into layer underneath, in first ch of foundation row, and work 1 sc. Continue the same way across row.

Rows 11–16: 1 sc in each st (48).

Now begin forming the clouds, making sure you understand how to crochet bobbles and how to make color changes.

NOTES

- All bobble stitches are worked on WS.
- All color changes are made as a sharp color change—that is, you should finish the stitch before the color change (the last stitch of the original color) by bringing the new color through on the last step of that stitch.
- When crocheting rows on RS, be aware of color changes, and also be aware whether or not you need to bring along color B for a couple of stitches (*you'll do this by simply crocheting around the strands of color B*), so that color B is already there and ready to be worked for the next row of bobbles.
- Divide the yarn (color B) for the clouds into two separate balls so that you won't need to take color B back and forth between the clouds.
- When you work with the bobble color, always work around color A (*crocheting around the strands of color A*)
- ⇒ means that you should change colors.

I recommend following the chart from this point on, but if you are in doubt, the instructions for the rows of bobbles are written out here.

Row 17: 10 sc ⇒ B, 3 x [1 bobble, 1 sc] ⇒ A, 16 sc ⇒ B, 3 x [1 bobble, 1 sc] ⇒ A, 10 sc.

Row 18: 10 sc ⇒ B, 6 sc ⇒ A, crochet around color B on next 2 sc, 14 sc ⇒ B, 6 sc ⇒ A, crochet around color B on next 2 sc, 8 sc.

Row 19: 8 sc ⇒ B, 5 x [1 bobble, 1 sc] ⇒ A, 12 sc ⇒ B, 5 x [1 bobble, 1 sc] ⇒ A, 8 sc.

Row 20: 8 sc → B, 10 sc → A, crochet around color B on next 2 sc, 10 sc → B, 10 sc → A, crochet around color B on next 2 sc, 6 sc.

Row 21: 6 sc → B, 7 x [1 bobble, 1 sc] → A, 8 sc → B, 7 x [1 bobble, 1 sc] → A, 6 sc.

Row 22: 8 sc → B, 6 sc → A, 2 sc → B, 4 sc → A, 8 sc → B, 4 sc → A, 2 sc → B, 6 sc → A, 8 sc.

Row 23: 8 sc → B, 3 x [1 bobble, 1 sc]→ A, 2 sc → B, 2 x [1 bobble, 1 sc] → A, 8 sc → B, 2 x [1 bobble, 1 sc] → A, 2 sc → B, 3 x [1 bobble, 1 sc] → A, 8 sc.

Row 24: 10 sc → B, 2 sc → A, 24 sc → B, 2 sc → A, 10 sc.

Row 25: 10 sc → B, 1 bobble, 1 sc → A, 24 sc → B, 1 bobble, 1 sc → A, 10 sc.

Rows 26–56: 1 sc in each st across.

Once you've crocheted the last row, wait to cut yarn.

Ch 1, turn work, and fold top edge down.

Now join for the top casing with a row of slip stitches on WS. Insert hook under both stitch loops of last sc that you worked. Next, insert hook 10 rows below (*marked with blue line on chart*), yarn over hook and bring yarn through both layers and the loops on the hook.

Continue the same way across row.

Cut yarn, fasten off, and weave in ends on WS.

PANEL CHART

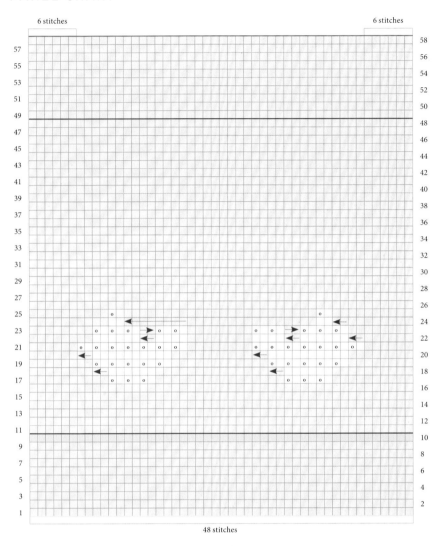

6 stitches

6 stitches

48 stitches

☐ Sc with color A

▨ Sc with color A where you join the foundation chain for bottom casing (fold bottom edge up on WS and work across on RS with sc).

○ Bobble with color B

☐ Sc with color B

◄► Crochet around the color not in use.

——— Work accent line on RS with slip stitches.

——— Slip stitch accent line and hanging cord worked on RS (but first after the crocheted casing at top).

——— Slip stitches with color A, where you worked top casing join, 10 rows below and marked with blue line (*fold top edge down on WS and work sl sts on WS*).

EMBROIDERY

Once you've made the panel, you can embroider the rainbow with cross stitches. Follow the chart shown here.

You don't need to worry about doing this correctly or about making neat stitches with a tidy look on the back of the panel. I just knotted the ends or sewed them around the thread ends. I would, though, recommend that you make the stitches in the same orientation, so that all the underneath stitches are on the same diagonal and all the top stitches are on the other diagonal. Your eyes will thank you for this cleaner look.

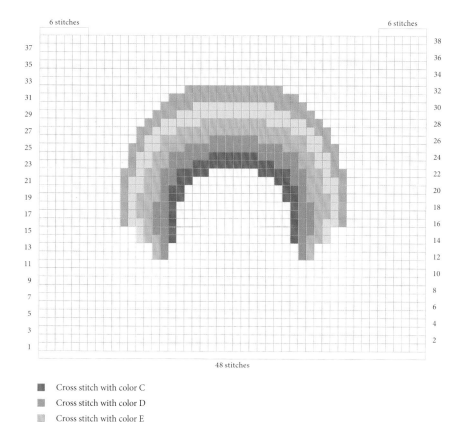

■ Cross stitch with color C
▨ Cross stitch with color D
▨ Cross stitch with color E
▨ Cross stitch with color F
▨ Cross stitch with color G

ACCENT LINE AND HANGING CORD

Work with your choice of color. I used color G.

Work 1 row of slip stitches (on RS) in the same place where you joined layers for casing (*marked with green line on chart*). There should be 6 rows between the slip stitch line and the beginning of the rainbow.

When you've crocheted all the way across, continue with ch 60–70, cut yarn, and fasten off. Tie the two loose ends together and weave in ends on WS.

Crochet another row of slip stitches the same way (*on RS*) at bottom of panel over casing line (*marked with red line on chart*). There should be 6 rows between the slip stitch line and the beginning of the clouds.

FINISHING

- Gently steam-press the tapestry under a damp pressing cloth. This will make a big difference and allow the stitches and embroidery to lie nice and flat.

- Insert a dowel through each casing.

- Finally, twist the hanging cord once around the dowel end at each side so the cord lies on the back side of the panel. This way, the piece will lie flat against the wall when hung up.

PLAY WINGS

If you want to add the most spectacular play wings to a child's dress-up box, these are the ones. They're full of gorgeous details and are well thought out for comfort. They are designed so that you don't need a sewing machine, but some hand sewing is required. It's not a difficult project, but it is a big project, and some steps require a bit of patience. Don't be intimidated by how many sections this project contains. This setup is just to make it easy to manage the various invisible seams and joins to create the best possible final result. Read through the entire pattern before getting started, then review each section as you tackle it. I am positive that you'll create wings to make any child happy.

SIZES

One size—the shoulder straps can be adjusted for best fit.

The wings measure approx. 28¾ in (73 cm) from wing tip to wing tip.
The center circle on each wing measures approx. 4¼ in (11 cm) in diameter.
Wing 1 (the narrow top wing) measures approx. 5¾ in (14.5 cm) at its widest point (at the circle motif) and approx. 13¾ in (35 cm) in length.
Wing 2 (the wide bottom wing) measures approx. 6¾ in (17 cm) at its widest point (at the circle motif) and approx. 11 in (28 cm) in length.
The circular back piece measures approx. 7 in (18 cm) in diameter.

CROCHET HOOK

U.S. D-3 (3 mm) and G-6 (4 mm)

YARN

Center Circle
Color C1: small amount Organic Cotton
Color C2: small amount Organic Cotton
Color C3: 25 g Organic Cotton
Color C4: 50 g Organic Cotton
Color C5: small amount Shiny

Wings 1 and 2
Color W1: 50 g Organic Cotton
Color W2: 50 g Organic Cotton

Edging 2 and Accent Lines
Color E: 25 g Shiny

Back
Color B1: 50 g Organic Cotton
Color B2: 25 g Shiny

NOTES

To ensure that the finished set of wings is both neat and sturdy, you'll need to use both interlining and interfacing (*Vlieseline and Vliesofix*), which means some ironing will be required. The fabric and yarn you use must therefore be heat tolerant. Test to make sure that your glitter yarn is heat tolerant before you begin working. I have never had any problems with the Glimmer yarn from Krea Deluxe (*80% viscose, 20% polyester*).

NOTIONS

- Stiff interlining (*Vlieseline*), H 250 with 1 glue side, 15¾ x 32½ in (40 x 80 cm)
- Interfacing (*Vliesofix*), 15¾ x 32½ in (40 x 80 cm)
- Firmly woven cotton fabric, 15¾ x 32½ in (40 x 80 cm)
- Elastic, approx. 1½ in (38–40 mm) wide, 47¼ in (120 cm) long (*look for "soft glitter elastic," "glitter elastic for pants," "boxer short elastic," etc.*)
- Sewing thread (*to match elastic*)
- 12 sew-on snaps, ¼ in (9 mm) (*only required if the back straps need to be adjusted*)

GAUGE

No gauge is listed, since it is difficult to calculate because there are several types of stitches and you will shift between rows and rounds. It is, therefore, most important that the crocheted fabric be neither too loose nor too firm and that you get close to the given measurements.

CONSTRUCTION

An abbreviated step-by-step summary is listed below; the individual steps will be described in much greater detail within the individual instruction sections.

- Begin by crocheting 2 x wing 1s (narrow), 2 x wing 2s (wide), and 1 x back.
- Iron stiff interlining on all the pieces.
- Outline shapes on interfacing.
- Iron interfacing onto fabric.
- Cut out fabric pieces and trim.
- Iron fabric to wing 1.
- Crochet wings together in pairs.
- Iron fabric to wing 2.
- Crochet wing pairs securely to back.
- Sew wide elastic straps to back.
- Sew snaps onto elastic and then back.
- Sew on a strap to hold elastic.
- Sew elastic straps securely on top of wing 1.
- Iron fabric onto back.
- Sew a piece of wide elastic on underside of each wing 1 for fitting around arm.

NOTES

- Work all single crochet as Y-single crochet stitches.
- Work rounds in a spiral.

4 X CENTER CIRCLES

Crochet hook: U.S. D-3 (3 mm).

Begin by crocheting 4 individual center circles for the four wings.

Color C1

Rnd 1: Make a magic ring and work 6 sc around ring (6).

Rnd 2: 6 Iinc (12).

Rnd 3: 6 x [1 sc, 1 Iinc], 1 sc (*to shift beginning of rnd here and for rest of pattern*) (18).

Rnd 4: 6 x [2 sc, 1 Iinc], SCC (24).

Color C2

Rnd 5: 6 x [3 sc, 1 Iinc], CR (30).

Rnd 6: 6 x [4 sc, 1 Iinc], SCC (36).

Color C3

Rnd 7: 6 x [1 sc, 1 Lsc into st 2 rows below (*in same place as you worked Rnd 4*), 1 sc, 1 Lsc 1 st to right and 2 rows below (*in st at side of first Lsc*), 1 sc, 1 Iinc], CR (42).

Rnd 8: 6 x [6 sc, 1 Iinc], SCC (48).

Color C4

Rnd 9: 2 sc, 1 Lsc 2 rows below (*in same place as you worked Rnd 7*), 3 sc, 1 Iinc, 5 x [3 sc, 1 Lsc 2 rows below (*in same place as you worked Rnd 7*), 3 sc, 1 Iinc], 1 sc (54).

Rnd 10: 6 x [8 sc, 1 Iinc], 1 sc (*to shift beginning of rnd here and for rest of pattern*) (60).

Rnd 11: 6 x [9 sc, 1 Iinc], 1 sc (66).

Rnd 12: 6 x [10 sc, 1 Iinc], 1 sc (72).

Rnd 13: 6 x [11 sc, 1 Iinc], 1 sc (78).

Rnd 14: 6 x [12 sc, 1 Iinc], 1 sc (84).

Rnd 15: 6 x [13 sc, 1 Iinc], 1 sc (90).

Rnd 16: 6 x [14 sc, 1 Iinc], 1 sc (96).

Cut yarn but do not fasten off; instead, just make the loop a bit longer, remove hook from loop, and let it rest. Before you make the next color change, embroider as follows:

- With color C5, embroider from the center and out in each stitch 3 rnds farther out.
- Knot yarns together on WS and weave in ends (*except for the last one*).

Now continue crocheting to turn each circle into a wing.

2 X WING 1S
(NARROW)

Make 2 x wing 1s (*narrow*) with color W1.

Take a center circle and attach yarn as you would for a SCC at the resting loop.

Color W1

Rnd 17: 6 x [15 sc, 1 Iinc], 1 sc (102).

Rnd 18: 6 x [16 sc, 1 Iinc], 1 sc (108).

Do not cut yarn; it is time to begin the point of the wing.

NOTES

- Work in rows from this point on.
- Also, from this point on, work decreases and increases like normal, not as invisible decreases and increases.
- Turn all rows with ch 1.

Row 1 (RS): 1 dec, 14 sc, 2 inc, 14 sc, 1 dec (34).

Now work in back loops only.

Row 2 (WS): 1 dec in bl, 14 sc in bl, 2 inc in bl, 14 sc in bl, 1 dec in bl (34).

Row 3 (RS): 1 dec in bl, 14 sc in bl, 2 inc in bl, 14 sc in bl, 1 dec in bl (34).

Row 4 (WS): 1 dec in bl, 14 sc in bl, 2 inc in bl, 14 sc in bl, 1 dec in bl (34).

Rows 5–40: Repeat Rows 3–4 (34).

Now revert to working through both stitch loops.

Row 41 (RS): 1 dec, 14 sc, 2 inc, 14 sc, 1 dec (34).

Do not cut yarn; continue to Edging 1.

2 X WING 2S
(WIDE)

Make 2 x wing 2s (*wide*) with colors W1 and W2.

Take a center circle and attach yarn as you would for a SCC at the resting loop.

Color W1

Rnd 17: 6 x [15 sc, 1 Iinc], CR (102).

Rnd 18: 1 sc, 6 x [16 sc, 1 Iinc], SCC (108).

Color W2

Rnd 19: 6 x [17 sc, 1 Iinc], CR (114).

Rnd 20: 6 x [18 sc, 1 Iinc], 1 sc (120).

Rnd 21: 6 x [19 sc, 1 Iinc], 1 sc (126).

Rnd 22: 6 x [20 sc, 1 Iinc] (132).

Do not cut yarn; it is time to begin the point of the wing.

NOTES

- Work in rows from this point on.
- Also, from this point on, work decreases and increases like normal, not as invisible decreases and increases.
- Turn all rows with ch 1.

Row 1 (RS): 1 dec, 18 sc, 2 inc, 18 sc, 1 dec (42).

Now work in back loops only.

Row 2 (WS): 1 dec in bl, 18 sc in bl, 2 inc in bl, 18 sc in bl, 1 dec in bl (42).

Row 3 (RS): 1 dec in bl, 18 sc in bl, 2 inc in bl, 18 sc in bl, 1 dec in bl (42).

Row 4 (WS): 1 dec in bl, 18 sc in bl, 2 inc in bl, 18 sc in bl, 1 dec in bl (42).

Rows 5–20: Repeat Rows 3–4 (42).

Now revert to working through both stitch loops.

Row 21 (RS): 1 dec, 18 sc, 2 inc, 18 sc, 1 dec (42).

Do not cut yarn; continue to Edging 1.

EDGING 1

Edging 1 is worked with the same color as each wing and creates a neat connection between the center circle portion and the skinnier wing portion of each wing. Continue to work around the entire wing in sc—crochet down along the edge of the wing portion, around the circle, and back along the wing portion's other edge. Do not crochet over the point again (*corresponding to Row 41 of wing 1 and Row 21 of wing 2*).

Work 1 sc per row/stitch (*when you come to the first place where the wing portion meets the circle, you will have a softer transition if you work 1 extra sc in the same place as the last sc on Row 1, where you crocheted it together with the next sc of the circle*).

There should be approx. 188 sts per round on wing 1 (*including the sts of Row 41*).

There should be approx. 172 sts per round on wing 2 (*including the sts of Row 21*).

You do not need to have this precise number of stitches, but try to find a repeating sequence for crocheting the sc around the edge so that the result will be uniform. If needed, you can make a couple of extra stitches at the point and corners if they are curling a little.

When you've worked all the way around, cut yarn and fasten off.

Make an invisible finishing join and weave in ends.

Now you can continue to Edging 2.

EDGING 2

Crochet hook: U.S. D-3 (3 mm).

Crochet an extra round of edging around all four wings for an especially pretty finish and to create a unifying look between the four wings.

Color E

- Make a slip knot and crochet a round of sc with 1 sc in each st. You can decide where to begin—I prefer starting at one of the two "corners" out on the tip.
- When you've worked all the way around, work another round with 1 sl st in each sc (*through both st loops*).
- Cut yarn and fasten off.
- Make an invisible finishing join and weave in ends on WS.

ACCENT LINES

Crochet hook: U.S. D-3 (3 mm).

You can now crochet accent lines on all four wings. These lines will add an extra-sharp finished feel and emphasize the details such as the circles. The accent lines are worked as sl sts and use the method described below.

The first accent line is worked with the same color as its wing.

- Make a slip knot, remove hook from loop, and let loop rest.
- With RS facing, insert hook into the same place as when you crocheted edging 2 with color E.
- Place loop back on hook and bring loop through to RS.
- Work 1 sl st in each st (*in the same place as when you crocheted sc for edging 1*).
- Crochet all the way around (*the last sl st is worked in the same place as loop you took up*).
- Cut yarn and fasten off.
- Make an invisible finishing join and weave in ends on WS.
- With color E, make another accent line on wing 1 and two lines on wing 2.
- On wing 1, crochet the accent line in the same place as for first round in color W1.
- On wing 2, crochet both an accent line in the same place as for first round in color W1, and in the same place as for the first round in color W2.

BACK

Crochet hook: U.S. G-6 (4 mm).

The back is worked with two strands held together: one each of Organic Cotton and Shiny.

Colors B1 and B2

Rnd 1: Make a magic ring and work 6 sc around it (6).

Rnd 2: 6 Iinc (12).

Rnd 3: 6 x [1 sc, 1 Iinc], 1 sc (*to shift beginning of rnd here and for rest of pattern*) (18).

Rnd 4: 6 x [2 sc, 1 Iinc], 1 sc (24).

Rnd 5: 6 x [3 sc, 1 Iinc], 1 sc (30).

Rnd 6: 6 x [4 sc, 1 Iinc], 1 sc (36).

Rnd 7: 6 x [5 sc, 1 Iinc], 1 sc (42).

Rnd 8: 6 x [6 sc, 1 Iinc], 1 sc (48).

Rnd 9: 6 x [7 sc, 1 Iinc], 1 sc (54).

Rnd 10: 6 x [8 sc, 1 Iinc], 1 sc (60).

Rnd 11: 6 x [9 sc, 1 Iinc], 1 sc (66).

Rnd 12: 6 x [10 sc, 1 Iinc], 1 sc (72).

Rnd 13: 6 x [11 sc, 1 Iinc], 1 sc (78).

Rnd 14: 6 x [12 sc, 1 Iinc], 1 sc (84).

Rnd 15: 6 x [13 sc, 1 Iinc], 1 sc (90).

Rnd 16: 6 x [14 sc, 1 Iinc], 1 sc (96).

Rnd 17: 6 x [15 sc, 1 Iinc], 1 sc (102).

Rnd 18: 1 sc in each st around (102).

Rnd 19: 1 sl st in each st around (102).

After completing the last round, remove hook from loop and let loop rest. Insert hook from WS under both stitch loops of next st. Place resting loop back on hook and bring through to WS. Remove hook from loop and let loop rest. Insert hook under both stitch loops of next st. Place loop back on hook and bring through to RS. You can now continue to work 1 sl st in each st around.

Cut yarn and fasten off.

Make an invisible finishing join and weave in ends on WS.

IRONING

Gently steam-press the four wings and the back under a damp pressing cloth so they will be nice and even. If needed, manipulate the pieces and edges for neatness and roundness.

STIFF INTERLINING

Now iron on the stiff interlining to each wing and the back. This helps each piece retain its shape and will make the rest of the finishing easier.

Work as follows:

- Lay the interlining on each piece (*with glue side facing WS of crochet piece*) and trace an outline about ⅜ in (1 cm) in all the way around. It does not need to be precise.
- Lay the interlining with glue side facing WS of each piece and iron on (*without steam*). Hold the iron over each piece for about 5–8 seconds until the interlining is firmly attached.

FABRIC AND INTERFACING

Now join fabric pieces with interfacing as follows:

- Lay the interfacing with the paper side facing up.
- Place all your pieces over the interfacing with RS up. Make sure that all the pieces lie as closely together as possible (*but lay the wings so the centerlines are somewhat "perpendicular" on the interfacing—this will ensure that it will subsequently align with the thread direction of the fabric. This is especially important if the fabric is patterned*).
- Trace around the outermost edge of each piece (*but wait to cut anything out!*).
- Do not cut the individual pieces on your interfacing yet; rather, cut so you have one large piece of interfacing with all the pieces drawn on it.
- Lay this piece of interfacing on your fabric with the glue side facing the WS (*if there is a difference*), and iron it on. Hold the iron over the whole piece for about 5–8 seconds until the interfacing is firmly attached.
- Now cut out all the fabric pieces and lay each one together with its corresponding crochet piece. The fabric pieces should be a little larger than the crocheted pieces.
- Lay the paper side of your fabric pieces over the WS of the crocheted pieces.
- Now, very carefully, cut your fabric pieces so they lie one round in on the wing, such that edging 1 in color E can still be seen and isn't completely covered by the fabric.
- Do not iron the fabric of the fabric pieces to the two wing 2s or the back. These will be ironed on later when you are ready with the individual pieces for finishing; doing it then will allow you to hide the various stitching lines.
- Iron your fabric pieces on the two wing 1s. Remove the paper, lay the fabric with glue side facing the WS, and iron the fabric on securely with an iron (*but no steam*). Hold the iron over the whole piece for about 5–8 seconds until the fabric is firmly attached.

JOINING THE PAIRS OF WINGS

There are a total of two pairs of wings. Each pair includes one wing 1 and one wing 2.

Lay the wings together in pairs by placing the narrow wing 1s on top and the wide wing 2s underneath. One pair of wings should point to the right and the other pair should point to the left.

Now sew the each pair together to create two final halves/sides. When you sew, it is more important that the wings look neat when seen from the RS of wing 1, since the sewing on the WS of wing 2 will later be hidden by fabric.

To be consistent in where you will join the pieces, first place a few stitch markers.

Each point of the wing pieces goes, respectively, over 34 sts on wing 1 and 42 sts on wing 2.

When you look at the wings from the RS and with the tips facing upward, mark the center of the tip sts on the left/right side. I recommend placing markers in the stitch before/after so you hold the st to be sewn free.

Also place an extra marker in wing 2. When you look again at the wings from the RS and with the tips facing upward, there should be two rows of holes down along the center (*where you crocheted the increases*).

You should stitch down along the right/left rows of holes to and including approx. hole 13, so place a marker after that hole.

Lay wing 1 over wing 2 so the marked sts at each tip are over each other. The left/right side of the top tip should align with the hole edge on the underneath wing piece.

With color W1, stitch through both layers, sewing together over the 17 sts on wing 1. Sew down between the two slip st rnds in the same holes as you crocheted slip st rounds in color W1. I stitched up and down until I had sewn all 17 sts, and then I sewed up again so I could be certain that the seam was quite strong.

From this point, continue by sewing down along the right/left row of holes on wing 1 that follows the edge in the tip of wing 2. Once again, stitch up and down, but, in a few places, you should skip a st, so you sew only in the places where the yarn can imitate the strand of a stitch. You should also sew over the places where the Vs (stitch loops) make a line (*WS rows on wing 1*)—that way, your stitching will be hidden. Sew over all 21 sts at the tip of wing 2 (*I did not sew back here*).

Cut yarn, fasten off, and weave in ends.

Now iron on the fabric piece for wing 2 as previously described; this will hide the sewing.

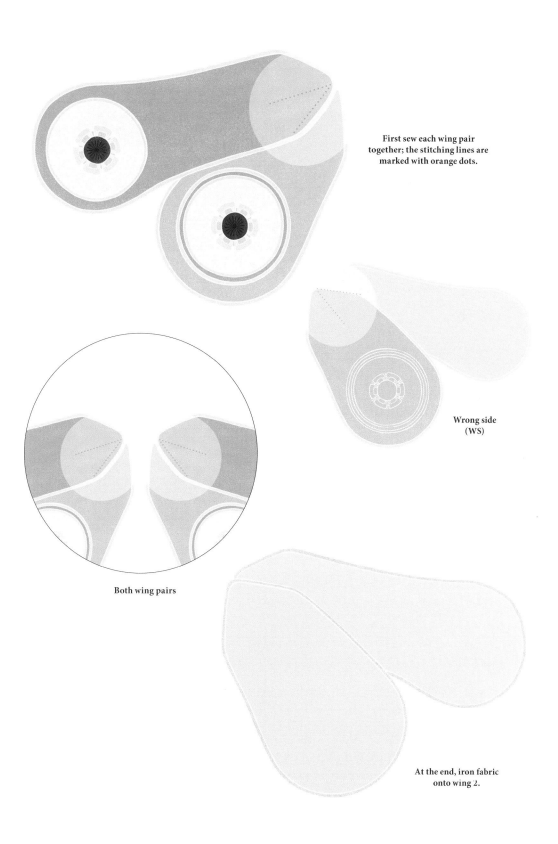

First sew each wing pair
together; the stitching lines are
marked with orange dots.

Wrong side
(WS)

Both wing pairs

At the end, iron fabric
onto wing 2.

JOINING THE WING PAIRS TO THE BACK

Now it's time to sew the wing pairs to the back.

Mark 6 sts at top of back to keep them free (*place markers before and after the 6 sts*). Lay wing pairs on the back so the marked sts at the tips frame the sts before and after the 6 top sts of the back. The line forming the marked 21 sts on left/right side of wing 2 should be perpendicular down from the tip so that it lies parallel with the corresponding line on the opposite pair of wings. It should align with the last marker sts framing about 4 rounds out from the center of the back (*where the lowest of the wings crosses the back circle—there should be about 20 sts between the wing pairs*). When the wing pairs are lying flat, about 20 sts are free below.

With color W2, sew through both layers of wing 2 and the back. Stitch over the 21 marked sts on wing 2—sew down along the accent line in the same color. I stitched up and down until I had sewn all 21 sts, and then I sewed up again so I could be certain that the seam was quite strong.

It is more important, when you are sewing, that it looks neat from the RS of wing 2, because the stitching on the WS of the back will subsequently be hidden by fabric.

Don't iron the fabric on the back yet!

LENGTH OF THE SHOULDER STRAPS

Next, cut two pieces of wide elastic to be used for the shoulder straps (*if you are using boxer shorts elastic, note the soft backing, which will be more comfortable against the skin*).

Snaps will be sewn on one end of the shoulder straps so you can adjust the length. This way, you can lengthen the lifespan of the wings so they can "grow" with the child and also be worn by children of different ages.

The length of the shoulder straps is measured from the top of the back and to the side of the back (*on the play wings, not the child!*).

If the elastic measures 15¾ in (40 cm), the shoulder straps will be, respectively, 9¾, 10¾, and 11½ in (25, 27, and 29 cm).

At their longest, the shoulder straps fit my five-year-old son, and, at their shortest, the straps fit my three-year-old daughter. Keep in mind, though, that not all children are the same height, so these are only recommendations. Calculate how long the shoulder straps should be at their shortest, add 5¼ in (13 cm),* and cut two pieces of elastic in that length.

*This leaves 1½ in (4 cm) for seaming (*⅜ in [1 cm] on one end and 1¼ in [3 cm] on the other end with double folds]*). The strap is placed about 2 in (5 cm) down from top back. At the side, the strap is 2½ in (6 cm) in over the back, when the strap is farthest in and thus shortest.

Of course, you can also choose to make the shoulder straps without snaps and simply sew both ends securely to the back. In that case, the elastic should be a bit shorter and not folded as many times.

Each wing pair is sewn to the back; the stitching lines are marked with orange dots.

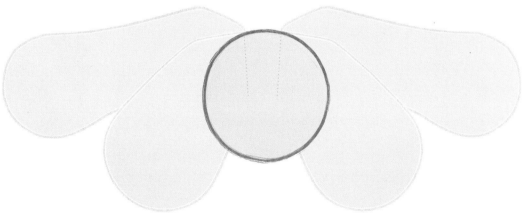

Wrong side (WS)

ATTACHING THE SHOULDER STRAPS

SNAPS TO STRAP

Fold one end of the elastic in twice (WS facing WS) so that the fold measures ⅝ in (1.5 cm) and there is room for sewing on the snaps.

Mark where two snaps will be attached before sewing them on. Fold the elastic out again and sew on snaps securely (*this way, you can hide your stitching from the snaps inside the fold afterward*).

Fold the end of the elastic together again and sew down with small stitches all the way around.

STRAP TO BACK

Place the opposite end of the elastic between the wings and back (*with WS facing RS of back*).

Fold the end of the elastic in once (*WS facing WS*) so that the fold measures ⅜ in (1 cm), and sew strap down securely so the end of the elastic is 2 in (5 cm) down on the side, furthest in to the center.

SNAPS TO BACK

Now sew snaps on RS of back.

Place the elastic so it aligns with the edge of the other end of the elastic.

Sew on two snaps to fit where the two ends will go "over" each other as well as two snaps close to the edge, where the corners of the two ends of elastic just reach each other.

Sew on the last two snaps securely between the others, equally spaced; in the end you should have approx. ¾ in (2 cm) between the three rows of snaps.

The shoulder straps lie between the wings and back.

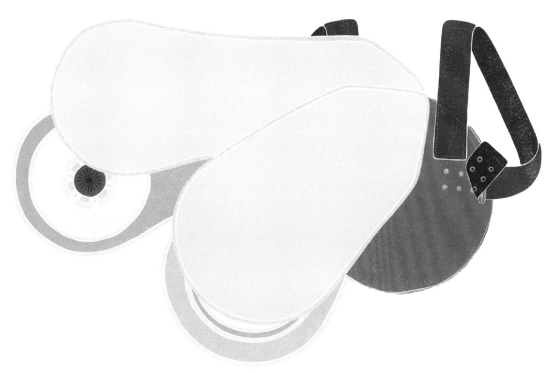

Note how the snaps are arranged and sewn on.

ADDING THE STRAP-SECURING LOOP

The idea here is that you are going to sew two large stitches over the elastic strap that will function as a simple loop that hold the elastic in place more securely. This way, the shoulder straps can be adjusted, and since the end with the snaps is thicker because of its two folds, it won't get pulled through by accident very easily.

First, place the elastic strap at the outermost snaps.

Hold together a strand each of Organic Cotton B1 and Shiny B2 and proceed as described:

- Attach the yarn to the edge of the back directly above the elastic.
- Bring the yarn down so it aligns with the stitching on the strap, then sew the first stitch on the back directly below the elastic so the stitch lies as close to the elastic as possible but doesn't crush it together or distort it.
- Bring the yarn back over the elastic and sew another stitch firmly on the other side.

ADDING EXTRA STITCHING AT THE TOP OF THE STRAP

Sew the elastic strap securely along the edge of wing 1 where the elastic overlaps it.

Use sewing thread for this, making sure you don't sew all the way through the wings, since you don't want it to be visible from the RS.

ADDING THE BACK FABRIC

Iron fabric on the back.

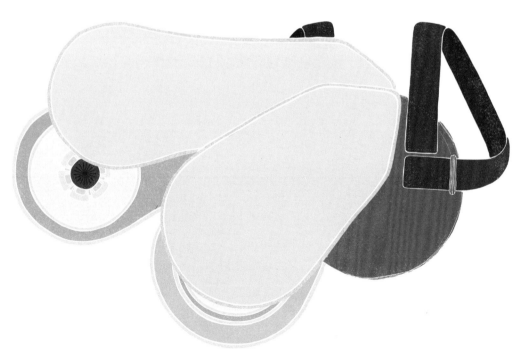

Note where the strap-securing loop is sewn on to help hold the elastic in place.

Here you can see the extra stitching added to the top
of the strap on wing 1.

Here's the ironed fabric on the back.

2 X ARM ELASTIC STRAPS

It's the final phase! It's time to attach an elastic strap on WS of each wing 1.

- Cut two pieces of wide elastic, each 6¼ in (16 cm) long.
- If your elastic has a tendency to unravel, sew over it with overhand stitches.
- Fold each end of the elastic under ⅜ in (1 cm) (*with WS facing WS*) and sew down securely.

Sew each elastic strap to a wing as follows:

- Place the strap so it lies as shown in the photo—the long edge of the elastic should be in the center of the circle and perpendicular to the center spine of the length of the wing.
- The elastic should lie so that the end's RS faces the WS of the wing—therefore, you need to fold the ends under one more time.
- Begin by sewing on one end. Use overhand stitch along the three outer sides of the folded portion, but don't sew down along the top edge of the folded portion. Also be careful not to sew all the way through the wing.
- Finally, sew just above the fold, but still hiding your stitches by sewing up in the fold, on the wrong side of the elastic. Again, be careful not to sew all the way through the wing.
- Sew the opposite end the same way. It can be a bit of a hassle to get in there properly, but simply push the elastic a little to the side so you have enough space to sew under.

The arm elastic straps are sewn to wing 1.

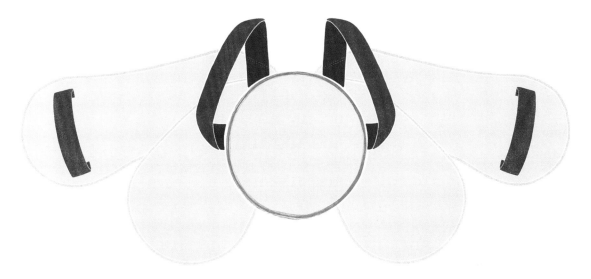

Arm elastic straps attached.

The finished wings from the RS.

HOBBYHORSE

A hobbyhorse is always a hit, but you can take it to a magical level by adding a glitter horn on its forehead. This project will teach you how to make an adventurous and sturdy unicorn, or, you can make a beautiful steed without a horn.

SIZES	One size
CROCHET HOOK	U.S. C-2 (2.5 mm), D-3 (3 mm), and G-6 (4 mm)
YARN	**Head** Color A: 250 g Wool 2 **Ears** Color A: Wool 2 (you'll have plenty from the head) Color B: Shiny (you'll have plenty from the horn) **Horn** Color B: 25 g Shiny **Eyes** Color C1 (*pupils and outlines*): small amount Organic Cotton Color C2 (*iris*): small amount Organic Cotton Color C3 (*shine on pupil*): small amount Shiny Color C4 (*shine on iris*): small amount Shiny Color C5 (*light reflection*): small amount Organic Cotton **Mane** Color D1: 75–100 g Organic Cotton and/or Shiny Color D2: small amount Shiny You can use as many colors as you'd like for the mane. I used a total of 75 g Organic Cotton plus a little Shiny.

- Fiberfill
- Round stick, ⅞ in (22 mm) circumference, 27½ in (70 cm) long
- 1 end cap, ⅞ in (22 mm) circumference

Halter *(optional)*
- Ribbon, approx. ½ –⅝ in (13–15 mm) wide,
- 37 in (94 cm) long *(for unicorn: without ribbon #7; see halter, page 175)*
- 44 in (112 cm) long *(for regular horse: with ribbon #7; see halter, page 175)*
- Sewing thread to match ribbon
- 2 keyrings, approx. 1 in (25 mm)
- 2 keyrings, approx. ¾ in (20 mm)

Reins *(optional)*
- Ribbon, approx. ⅝–¾ in (15–20 mm) wide, approx. 23¾ in (59 cm) long
- Sewing thread to match ribbon
- 2 carabiner clasps / keyrings with spring closure, 1¼ in (30 mm)

GAUGE

20 sts x 23 rows = 4 x 4 in (10 x 10 cm) crocheted in the round with hook U.S. G-6 (4 mm). Adjust hook size to obtain correct gauge if needed.

The gauge is not very important, so only the gauge for the head is given here. It is important, though, that the crochet be relatively firm, especially for the head, which you will fill with fiberfill. You want to be sure that the the gauge is tight enough that the fill won't show through the crocheted fabric.

CONSTRUCTION

- Begin by making the nostrils, ears, eyes, and horn.
- Next, make the base.
- Crochet the head starting from the nose and moving toward the neck, with gussets halfway.
- Fill the head with fiberfill.
- Attach the nostrils, ears, eyes, and horn to the head.
- A halter can be added to the head if desired.
- Finish the stick and mount it to the base.
- Crochet the head and base together.
- Finally, add and trim the mane.

2 X NOSTRILS

Crochet hook: U.S. G-6 (4 mm)

Color A

Rnd 1: Make a magic ring and work 6 sc around it (6).

Rnd 2: 6 Iinc (12).

Rnd 3: 6 x [1 sc, 1 Iinc], 1 sc (*to shift beginning of rnd here and for rest of pattern*) (18).

Rnd 4: 6 x [2 sc, 1 Iinc], 1 sc (24).

Cut yarn and fasten off, leaving an end long enough for sewing on nostril.

FINISHING

Fold each nostril at the middle and sew together with overhand stitch.

Do not attach yet.

2 X EARS

Crochet hook: U.S. G-6 (4 mm)

Color A

Rnd 1: Make a magic ring and work 6 sc around it (6).

Rnd 2: 1 sc in each st around (6).

Rnd 3: 2 x [1 Iinc, 1 sc, 1 Iinc] (10).

Rnd 4: 1 sc in each st around (10).

Rnd 5: 2 x [1 Iinc, 3 sc, 1 Iinc] (14).

Rnd 6: 1 sc in each st around (14).

Rnd 7: 2 x [1 Iinc, 5 sc, 1 Iinc] (18).

Rnd 8: 1 sc in each st around (18).

Rnd 9: 2 x [1 Iinc, 7 sc, 1 Iinc] (22).

Rnd 10: 1 sc in each st around (22).

Rnd 11: 2 x [1 Iinc, 9 sc, 1 Iinc] (26).

Rnd 12: 1 sc in each st around (26).

Rnd 13: 2 x [1 Iinc, 11 sc, 1 Iinc] (30).

Rnds 14–15: 1 sc in each st around (30).

Rnd 16: 2 x [1 Iinc, 13 sc, 1 Iinc] (34).

Rnds 17–18: 1 sc in each st around (34).

Rnd 19: 2 x [1 Idec, 13 sc, 1 Idec] (30).

Rnds 20–21: 1 sc in each st around (30).

Rnd 22: 2 x [1 Idec, 11 sc, 1 Idec] (26).

Rnds 23–24: 1 sc in each st around (26).

Cut yarn and fasten off, leaving an end long enough to join ear and attach it to head.

EAR FINISHING

- Because the ear will tend to draw in on itself a bit, it's a good idea to dampen it to make it easier to manipulate. This also helps the stitches lie as nicely as possible over each other.

- With color B, embroider the inside of the ear. Cut yarn, fasten off, and weave in ends on WS.

- Lay ear flat and sew together with overhand stitch.

- Fold each side of ear in toward center and sew together.

- Do not attach ears yet.

EARS CHART

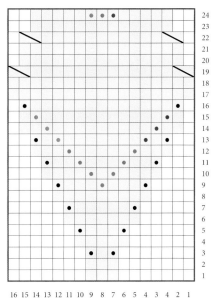

16 15 14 13 12 11 10 9 8 7 6 5 4 3 4 2 1

	Sc
•	Iinc
⟍	Idec
▯	Repeat once more.

EMBROIDERY

Embroider from the lowest point/stitch of each color on the ear to all the other points/stitches of the same color.

HORN

Crochet hook: U.S. D-3 (3 mm)

The horn is worked in a spiral, however it is not worked in traditional rounds. The last stitch will be moving and adjusting—more freeform, so you will be working some of the last stitches of a round into the next round. The last stitch you work will not always be on top of your last round's last stitch. In a way similar to a shift stitch, you will adjust the last stitch for these rounds.

NOTES

- Work all single crochet as X-single crochet stitches.
- Crochet around in a spiral.
- Don't forget to add fiberfill several times as you work.

TIPS

I suggest that you note down each time you have completed a round to help you keep track of how far you've come. It can get very hard to "see" the stitches in glitter yarn, where there are decreases and increases; it can also be tricky to count backward when the rounds are crocheted "over themselves" throughout.

Be especially careful when crocheting invisible decreases at the end of every round. The stitches can become pulled in and trick your eyes so it looks as if there is an extra stitch when you count. You might begin the next round one stitch too soon (*that is, in the same stitch as the last stitch, where you made the decrease*).

Color D

Rnd 1: Make a magic ring and work 5 sc around it (5).

Rnd 2: Work 1 sc in each st around (5).

Rnd 3: 1 Iinc, 4 sc (6).

Rnd 4: 1 sc, 2 Iinc, 2 sc, 1 Idec (7).

Rnd 5: 4 sc, 1 Iinc, 2 sc, 1 Idec (7).

Add a little fiberfill. From this point on, I recommend you add fiberfill after every other round.

Rnd 6: 3 sc, 2 Iinc, 2 sc, 1 Idec (8).

Rnd 7: 5 sc, 1 Iinc, 2 sc, 1 Idec (8).

Rnd 8: 4 sc, 2 Iinc, 2 sc, 1 Idec (9).

Rnd 9: 6 sc, 1 Iinc, 2 sc, 1 Idec (9).

Rnd 10: 5 sc, 2 Iinc, 2 sc, 1 Idec (10).

Rnd 11: 7 sc, 1 Iinc, 2 sc, 1 Idec (10).

Rnd 12: 6 sc, 2 Iinc, 2 sc, 1 Idec (11).

Rnd 13: 8 sc, 1 Iinc, 2 sc, 1 Idec (11).

Rnd 14: 7 sc, 2 Iinc, 2 sc, 1 Idec (12).

Rnd 15: 9 sc, 1 Iinc, 2 sc, 1 Idec (12).

Rnd 16: 8 sc, 2 Iinc, 2 sc, 1 Idec (13).

Rnd 17: 10 sc, 1 Iinc, 2 sc, 1 Idec (13).

Rnd 18: 9 sc, 2 Iinc, 2 sc, 1 Idec (14).

Rnd 19: 11 sc, 1 Iinc, 2 sc, 1 Idec (14).

Rnd 20: 10 sc, 2 Iinc, 2 sc, 1 Idec (15).

Rnd 21: 12 sc, 1 Iinc, 2 sc, 1 Idec (15).

Rnd 22: 11 sc, 2 Iinc, 2 sc, 1 Idec (16).

Rnd 23: 13 sc, 1 Iinc, 2 sc, 1 Idec (16).

Rnd 24: 12 sc, 2 Iinc, 2 sc, 1 Idec (17).

Rnd 25: 14 sc, 1 Iinc, 2 sc, 1 Idec (17).

Rnd 26: 13 sc, 2 Iinc, 2 sc, 1 Idec (18).

Rnd 27: 15 sc, 1 Iinc, 2 sc, 1 Idec (18).

Rnd 28: 14 sc, 2 Iinc, 2 sc, 1 Idec (19).

Rnd 29: 16 sc, 1 Iinc, 2 sc, 1 Idec (19).

Rnd 30: 15 sc, 2 Iinc, 2 sc, 1 Idec (20).

Rnd 31: 17 sc, 1 Iinc, 2 sc, 1 Idec (20).

Rnd 32: 16 sc, 2 Iinc, 2 sc, 1 Idec (21).

Rnd 33: 18 sc, 1 Iinc, 2 sc, 1 Idec (21).

Rnd 34: 17 sc, 2 Iinc, 2 sc, 1 Idec (22).

Rnd 35: 19 sc, 1 Iinc, 2 sc, 1 Idec (22).

Rnd 36: 18 sc, 2 Iinc, 2 sc, 1 Idec (23).

Rnd 37: 20 sc, 1 Iinc, 2 sc, 1 Idec (23).

Rnd 38: 19 sc, 2 Iinc, 2 sc, 1 Idec (24).

Rnd 39: 21 sc, 1 Iinc, 2 sc, 1 Idec (24).

Rnd 40: 20 sc, 2 Iinc, 2 sc, 1 Idec (25).

Rnd 41: 22 sc, 1 Iinc, 2 sc, 1 Idec (25).

Rnd 42: 1 sc in each st around (25).

The horn should measure approx. 5½ in (14 cm).

Cut yarn and fasten off, leaving an end long enough to sew on horn.

Do not attach horn yet.

LEFT EYE

Crochet hook: U.S. C-2 (2.5 mm)

PUPIL

Work first 3 rnds with sc as X-sc.

Color C1

Rnd 1: Make a magic ring and work 6 sc around it—but do not pull in ring too much, because you will later embroider in it (6).

Rnd 2: 6 Iinc (12).

Rnd 3: 6 x [1 sc, 1 Iinc], 1 sc (18).

Leave yarn hanging and change to color C2 (*color for iris*) with SCC.

NOTES

- From this point on, work single crochet as Y-single crochet stitches.
- On next rounds, alternate between slip sts, sc, and hdc.

IRIS

Rnd 4: 12 sl sts, 1 inc, 3 x [2 hdc in next st], 1 inc, 1 sl st (23).

Cut yarn and fasten off.

Make an invisible finishing join and weave in ends on WS.

Now insert hook into back loop of stitch before the last sl st of Rnd 4 and bring color C1 through on last step.

OUTLINE

Rnd 5: 10 sl st in bl, 1 sc in bl, in next st work (1 sc bl, 1 hdc bl, 1 sc bl), 1 sc bl, 7 sl sts bl, 1 sc bl, in next st, work (1 sc bl, 1 hdc bl, 1 sc bl), 1 sc bl (27).

Cut yarn and change to color C3 (*Shiny Black*) by bringing it through on last step of last sc on Rnd 5.

Rnd 6: 1 sl st in bl in each st except for the last 2 hdc (*1 on each side*), where you work the following (1 sl st bl, ch 1, 1 sl st bl) (29).

Cut yarn and fasten off, leaving a long-enough end of color C3 to attach and embroider the inside of the eye as well as eyelashes.

Make an invisible finishing join, drawing yarn to WS. Tie it with beginning end in color C3 with three knots; leave long end hanging.

Weave in other ends, then crochet right eye (*don't embroider until after both eyes are worked*).

RIGHT EYE

Crochet hook: U.S. C-2 (2.5 mm)

PUPIL

Work first 3 rnds with single crochet as X-single crochet stitches.

Color C1

Rnd 1: Make a magic ring and work 6 sc around it—but do not pull in ring too much because you will later embroider in it (6).

Rnd 2: 6 Iinc (12).

Rnd 3: 6 x [1 sc, 1 Iinc], 1 sc (18).

Leave yarn hanging and change to color C2 (*color for iris*) with SCC.

> ### NOTES
>
> - From this point on, work single crochet as Y-single crochet stitches.
> - On next round, alternate between slip sts, sc, and hdc.

IRIS

Rnd 4: 1 sl st, 2 sc in next st, 3 x [2 hdc in next st], 2 sc in next st, 12 sl sts (23).

Cut yarn and fasten off.

Make an invisible finishing join and weave in ends on WS.

Now insert hook into back loop of stitch after the last sl st of Rnd 4 and bring color C1 through on last step.

OUTLINE

Rnd 5: 1 sc in bl, in next st work (1 sc bl, 1 hdc bl, 1 sc bl), 1 sc bl, 7 sl sts bl, 1 sc bl, in next st, work (1 sc bl, 1 hdc bl, 1 sc bl), 1 sc bl, 10 sl st in bl (27).

Cut yarn and change to color C3 (*Shiny Black*) by bringing it through on last step of last sc on Rnd 5.

Rnd 6: 1 sl st in bl in each st except for the last 2 hdc (*1 on each side*), where you work the following (1 sl st bl, ch 1, 1 sl st bl) (29).

Cut yarn and fasten off, leaving a long-enough end of color C3 to attach and embroider the inside of the eye as well as eyelashes.

Make an invisible finishing join, drawing yarn to WS. Tie it with beginning end in color C3 with three knots; leave long end hanging.

Weave in other ends. Now you can embroider both eyes.

EMBROIDERING THE EYES

SHINE AROUND THE PUPILS

Use the loose ends of color C3.

Embroider from each of the 5 sts where you increased on Rnd 4 and into the center of the magic ring.

Once you've finished the embroidery, tighten the magic ring well, tie the end from the magic ring with the yarn end, and weave in ends.

STRIPED IRISES

Now embroider the glitter stripes in the irises.

Use one strand of color C4 to embroider stripes from each of the 5 sts where you increased on Rnd 4 and out to each of the 10 increase sts (= *10 small lines*).

Weave in ends on WS.

SMALL LIGHT REFLECTIONS

Embroider with one strand of color C5.

Remember, when you have finished the embroidery, do not cut the yarn, because you will embroider the large light reflections with the same strand.

Hold the eye so the two points are horizontal. The little light reflection in each eye should be in approximately the top center.

Sew twice around the transition from the iris to the outline and over 1 st.

LARGE LIGHT REFLECTIONS

Sew the large light reflection in each eye with 1 st in between it and the small light reflection. The large light reflections should be closer to the nose.

Sew three times around the transition from the iris to the outline and over 2 sts.

Don't finish yet.

BASE

Crochet hook: U.S. G-6 (4 mm)

NOTES

- Work all single crochet as X-single crochet stitches.
- From Rnd 3 on, work in a spiral.

Color A

Row 1: Ch 14 + ch 1 extra for turning (14).

Row 2: 1 sc in each st through the little loop on back of foundation chain (14).

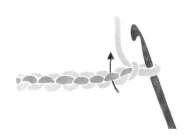

Continue in the round, beginning by working in the first sc of row.

Rnds 3–13: 1 sc in each st (14).

Rnd 14: 1 sc, 3 Iinc, 1 sc, 2 Iinc, 1 sc, 3 Iinc, 1 sc, 2 Iinc (24).

Rnd 15: 6 x [3 sc, 1 Iinc], 1 sc (*to shift beginning of rnd here and for rest of pattern*) (30).

Rnd 16: 6 x [4 sc, 1 Iinc], 1 sc (36).

Rnd 17: 6 x [5 sc, 1 Iinc], 1 sc (42).

Rnd 18: 6 x [6 sc, 1 Iinc], 1 sc (48).

Rnd 19: 6 x [7 sc, 1 Iinc], 1 sc (54).

Rnd 20: 6 x [8 sc, 1 Iinc], 1 sc (60).

Rnd 21: 6 x [9 sc, 1 Iinc], 1 sc (66).

Rnd 22: 6 x [10 sc, 1 Iinc], 1 sc (72).

Rnd 23: 6 x [11 sc, 1 Iinc], 1 sc (78).

Rnd 24: 1 sc in each st around (78).

Cut yarn, fasten off, and weave in ends.

With beginning yarn end, make an invisible finishing join on tube (*corresponding to Rnd 2*).

Weave in end.

EDGING ON BASE TUBE

Crochet hook: U.S. D-3 (3 mm)

Color D

Rnd 1: Make a slip st and work 2 sc in each st around the bottom of the base tube (28).

Rnd 2: 1 sl st in each st (through both loops) (28).

Cut yarn and fasten off.

Make an invisible finishing join and weave in ends.

HEAD

Crochet hook: U.S. G-6 (4 mm)

NOTES

- Work all single crochet as X-single crochet stitches.
- Work around in a spiral.

TIP

I recommend that you note down each time you've crocheted a round to help you keep track of how far you've come.

Color A

Rnd 1: Make a magic ring and work 6 sc around it (6).

Rnd 2: 6 Iinc (12).

Rnd 3: 6 x [1 sc, 1 Iinc], 1 sc (*to shift beginning of rnd here and for rest of pattern*) (18).

Rnd 4: 6 x [2 sc, 1 Iinc], 1 sc (24).

Rnd 5: 6 x [3 sc, 1 Iinc], 1 sc (30).

Rnd 6: 6 x [4 sc, 1 Iinc], 1 sc (36).

Rnd 7: 6 x [5 sc, 1 Iinc], 1 sc (42).

Rnd 8: 6 x [6 sc, 1 Iinc], 1 sc (48).

Rnds 9–18: 1 sc in each st around (48).

Rnd 19: 1 Idec, 6 x [2 sc, 1 Idec], 1 sc in each st to end of rnd (41).

Rnd 20: 6 x [1 sc, 1 Idec], 1 sc in each st to end of rnd (35).

Rnd 21: 1 sc in each st to end of rnd (35).

Rnd 22: 6 x [1 sc, 1 Iinc], 1 sc in each st to end of rnd (41).

Rnd 23: 1 sc in each st, 1 sc (*to shift beginning of rnd here and for rest of pattern*) (41).

Rnd 24: 7 sc, 1 Iinc, 3 sc, 1 Iinc, 1 sc in each st to end of rnd (43).

Rnds 25–26: 1 sc in each st around (43).

Rnd 27: 7 sc, 1 Iinc, 5 sc, 1 Iinc, 1 sc in each st to end of rnd (45).

Rnds 28–29: 1 sc in each st around (45).

Rnd 30: 7 sc, 1 Iinc, 7 sc, 1 Iinc, 14 sc, 1 Iinc, 6 sc, 1 Iinc, 7 sc (49).

Rnds 31–32: 1 sc in each st around (49).

Rnd 33: 7 sc, 1 Iinc, 2 sc, 1 Iinc, 3 sc, 1 Iinc, 2 sc, 1 Iinc, 15 sc, 1 Iinc, 6 sc, 1 Iinc, 8 sc (55).

Rnd 34: 1 sc in each st around (55).

Rnd 35: 7 sc, 1 Iinc, 3 sc, 1 Iinc, 5 sc, 1 Iinc, 3 sc, 1 Iinc, 15 sc, 1 Iinc, 8 sc, 1 Iinc, 8 sc (61).

Rnd 36: 1 sc in each st around (61).

Rnd 37: 1 sc, 1 Iinc, 3 x [2 sc, 1 Iinc], 11 sc, 1 Iinc, 3 x [2 sc, 1 Iinc], 10 sc, 1 Iinc, 8 sc, 1 Iinc, 9 sc (71).

Rnd 38: 1 sc in each st around (71).

Rnd 39: 16 sc, 1 Idec, 5 sc, 1 Idec, 1 sc in each st to end of rnd (69).

Rnd 40: 1 sc, 1 Iinc, 2 x [3 sc, 1 Iinc], 19 sc, 1 Iinc, 2 x [3 sc, 1 Iinc], 11 sc, 1 Iinc, 8 sc, 1 Iinc, 10 sc (77).

Rnd 41: 18 sc, 1 Idec, 6 sc, 1 Idec, 1 sc in each st to end of rnd (75).

Rnd 42: 1 sc in each st around (75).

Rnd 43: 1 sc, 1 Idec, 7 sc, 1 Idec, 4 sc, 1 Idec, 6 sc, 1 Idec, 4 sc, 1 Idec, 7 sc, 1 Idec, 1 sc in each st to end of rnd (69).

Rnds 44–45: 1 sc in each st around (69).

Rnd 46: 1 sc, 1 Idec, 5 sc, 1 Idec, 4 sc, 1 Idec, 5 sc, 1 Idec, 4 sc, 1 Idec, 5 sc, 1 Idec, 1 sc in each st to end of rnd (63).

Rnds 47–48: 1 sc in each st around, 1 sc (63).

Rnd 49: 41 sc, 1 Idec, 8 sc, 1 Idec, 10 sc (61).

Rnd 50: 1 sc in each st around (61).

On next rnd, use the two loose ends as markers before and after the bottom 14 sts at neck.

Rnd 51: 11 sc (*place marker*), 1 Iinc, 4 x [1 sc, 1 Iinc] (*place marker*), 1 sc in each st end of rnd (66).

Rnd 52: 45 sc, 1 Idec, 8 sc, 1 Idec, 9 sc (64).

End with 1 sl st in next st, cut yarn and fasten off.

Now make four gussets. After each gusset, work two "in-between rounds."

The following notes apply to all four gussets (*and this information is not written into the instructions, so take special note*).

NOTES ON GUSSETS

- All rows are worked on RS.
- Each time you crochet a new row, begin with a slip st.
- When you have worked the last st on a row, cut yarn and draw yarn end to WS.
- The following row always begins 2 sts after beginning of previous row and ends 2 sts before end of previous row.
- The stitch counts in gray within parentheses now refer to the stitch count of the row and not to the entire round.

GUSSET 1

Gusset 1 is worked over 50 sts while the lower 14 sts, marked on Rnd 51, are kept free—the first st to be crocheted into is the st after these 14 sts.

Row 1: 1 sl st in bl, 48 sc, 1 sl st in bl (50).

Row 2: 1 sl st in bl, 16 sc, 1 Idec, 8 sc, 1 Idec, 16 sc, 1 sl st in bl (44).

Row 3: 1 sl st in bl, 38 sc, 1 sl st in bl (40).

Row 4: 1 sl st in bl, 11 sc, 1 Idec, 8 sc, 1 Idec, 11 sc, 1 sl st in bl (34).

Row 5: 1 sl st in bl, 28 sc, 1 sl st in bl (30).

Row 6: 1 sl st in bl, 6 sc, 1 Idec, 8 sc, 1 Idec, 6 sc, 1 sl st in bl (24).

Row 7: 1 sl st in bl, 18 sc, 1 sl st in bl (20).

Row 8: 1 sl st in bl, 1 sc, 1 Idec, 8 sc, 1 Idec, 1 sc, 1 sl st in bl (14).

Now crochet the "in-between rounds," working all the way around the head.

NOTES ON IN-BETWEEN ROUNDS

The slip stitches crocheted at the beginning and end of the gusset rows are made to avoid any holes that might occur. You should imagine that these stitches are not "there" when you crochet sc all the way around. That is, when you come to the place where you crocheted the slip stitch, you should crochet around it (= *crochet through both stitch loops of the same stitch that the slip stitch was made in; this way, it will be hidden*).

IN-BETWEEN ROUND 1

The yarn is attached at the top of the head, in the fifth of the 8 sc at center.

Rnd 53: 23 sc, 1 Iinc, 3 x [2 sc, 1 Iinc], 23 sc (60).

Rnd 54: 4 sc, 1 Idec, 48 sc, 1 Idec, 4 sc (58).

End with 1 sl st in bl, cut yarn, and fasten off.

Tie the loose ends from the short row in pairs. You do not need to weave these in—just trim them a little shorter so they don't bother you as you continue to crochet.

GUSSET 2

Gusset 2 is worked over 50 sts while the lower 8 sts at neck are kept free—the first st to be crocheted into is the st after these 8 sts.

Row 1: 1 sl st in bl, 48 sc, 1 sl st in bl (50).

Row 2: 1 sl st in bl, 16 sc, 1 Idec, 8 sc, 1 Idec, 16 sc, 1 sl st in bl (44).

Row 3: 1 sl st in bl, 38 sc, 1 sl st in bl (40).

Row 4: 1 sl st in bl, 11 sc, 1 Idec, 8 sc, 1 Idec, 11 sc, 1 sl st in bl (34).

Row 5: 1 sl st in bl, 28 sc, 1 sl st in bl (30).

Row 6: 1 sl st in bl, 6 sc, 1 Idec, 8 sc, 1 Idec, 6 sc, 1 sl st in bl (24).

Row 7: 1 sl st in bl, 18 sc, 1 sl st in bl (20).

Row 8: 1 sl st in bl, 1 sc, 1 Idec, 8 sc, 1 Idec, 1 sc, 1 sl st in bl (14).

IN-BETWEEN ROUND 2

The yarn is attached at the top of the head, in the fifth of the 8 sc at center.

Rnd 55: 21 sc, 8 Iinc, 21 sc (58).

Rnd 56: 4 sc, 1 Idec, 46 sc, 1 Idec, 4 sc (56).

End with 1 sl st in bl, cut yarn, and fasten off.

Tie the loose ends from the short row in pairs. You do not need to weave these in—just trim them a little shorter so they don't bother you as you continue to crochet.

GUSSET 3

Gusset 3 is worked over 50 sts while the lower 6 sts at neck are kept free—the first st to be crocheted into is the st after these 6 sts.

Row 1: 1 sl st in bl, 48 sc, 1 sl st in bl (50).

Row 2: 1 sl st in bl, 16 sc, 1 Idec, 8 sc, 1 Idec, 16 sc, 1 sl st in bl (44).

Row 3: 1 sl st in bl, 38 sc, 1 sl st in bl (40).

Row 4: 1 sl st in bl, 11 sc, 1 Idec, 8 sc, 1 Idec, 11 sc, 1 sl st in bl (34).

Row 5: 1 sl st in bl, 28 sc, 1 sl st in bl (30).

Row 6: 1 sl st in bl, 6 sc, 1 Idec, 8 sc, 1 Idec, 6 sc, 1 sl st in bl (24).

Row 7: 1 sl st in bl, 18 sc, 1 sl st in bl (20).

Row 8: 1 sl st in bl, 1 sc, 1 Idec, 8 sc, 1 Idec, 1 sc, 1 sl st in bl (14).

IN-BETWEEN ROUND 3

The yarn is attached at the top of the head, in the fifth of the 8 sc at center.

Rnd 57: 21 sc, 6 Iinc, 21 sc (54).

Rnd 58: 4 sc, 1 Idec, 42 sc, 1 Idec, 4 sc (52).

End with 1 sl st in bl, cut yarn, and fasten off.

Tie the loose ends from the short row in pairs. You do not need to weave these in—just trim them a little shorter so they don't bother you as you continue to crochet.

GUSSET 4

Gusset 4 is worked over 40 sts while the lower 12 sts at neck are kept free—the first st to be crocheted into is the st after these 12 sts.

Row 1: 1 sl st in bl, 38 sc, 1 sl st in bl (40).

Row 2: 1 sl st in bl, 11 sc, 1 Idec, 8 sc, 1 Idec, 11 sc, 1 sl st in bl (34).

Row 3: 1 sl st in bl, 28 sc, 1 sl st in bl (30).

Row 4: 1 sl st in bl, 6 sc, 1 Idec, 8 sc, 1 Idec, 6 sc, 1 sl st in bl (24).

Row 5: 1 sl st in bl, 18 sc, 1 sl st in bl (20).

Row 6: 1 sl st in bl, 1 sc, 1 Idec, 8 sc, 1 Idec, 1 sc, 1 sl st in bl (14).

IN-BETWEEN ROUND 4

The yarn is attached at the top of the head, in the fifth of the 8 sc at center.

Rnd 59: 20 sc, 6 Iinc, 20 sc (52).

Rnd 60: 4 sc, 1 Idec, 40 sc, 1 Idec, 4 sc (50).

Do not cut yarn; instead, continue crocheting around neck. Begin on round now at top of head. Before you begin, first tie the loose ends together as you have been doing.

Tie the loose ends from the short row in pairs. You do not need to weave these in—just trim them a little shorter so they don't bother you as you continue to crochet.

NECK

Rnd 61: 1 sc in each st around (50).

Rnd 62: 21 sc, 1 Iinc, 6 sc, 1 Iinc, 21 sc (52).

Rnd 63: 1 sc in each st around (52).

Rnd 64: 22 sc, 1 Iinc, 6 sc, 1 Iinc, 22 sc (54).

Rnd 65: 1 sc in each st around, 1 sc (*to shift beginning of round here and for rest of pattern*) (52).

Rnd 66: 23 sc, 1 Iinc, 6 sc, 1 Iinc, 23 sc (56).

Rnd 67: 1 sc in each st around (56).

Rnd 68: 24 sc, 1 Iinc, 6 sc, 1 Iinc, 24 sc (58).

Rnd 69: 1 sc in each st around (58).

Rnd 70: 25 sc, 1 Iinc, 6 sc, 1 Iinc, 25 sc (60).

Rnd 71: 1 sc in each st around (60).

Rnd 72: 26 sc, 1 Iinc, 6 sc, 1 Iinc, 26 sc (62).

Rnd 73: 1 sc in each st around (62).

Rnd 74: 27 sc, 1 Iinc, 6 sc, 1 Iinc, 27 sc (64).

Rnd 75: 1 sc in each st around (64).

Rnd 76: 28 sc, 1 Iinc, 6 sc, 1 Iinc, 28 sc (66).

Rnd 77: 1 sc in each st around (66).

Rnd 78: 29 sc, 1 Iinc, 6 sc, 1 Iinc, 29 sc (68).

Rnd 79: 1 sc in each st around (68).

Rnd 80: 30 sc, 1 Iinc, 6 sc, 1 Iinc, 30 sc (70).

Rnd 81: 1 sc in each st around (70).

Rnd 82: 31 sc, 1 Iinc, 6 sc, 1 Iinc, 31 sc (72).

Rnd 83: 1 sc in each st around (72)

Rnd 84: 32 sc, 1 Iinc, 6 sc, 1 Iinc, 32 sc (74).

Rnd 85: 1 sc in each st around (74).

Rnd 86: 33 sc, 1 Iinc, 6 sc, 1 Iinc, 33 sc (76).

Rnd 87: 1 sc in each st around (76).

Rnd 88: 34 sc, 1 Iinc, 6 sc, 1 Iinc, 34 sc (78).

Rnd 89: 1 sc in each st around (78).

Cut yarn and fasten off, leaving an end long enough for attaching base.

FIBERFILL

Now fill the head with fiberfill. The head should be very well packed, but not so much that the fill is visible through the crocheted fabric.

Make sure you don't compact the fill as you stuff. Although you've crocheted with X-sc stitches, you will notice that the work still twists. Make sure that you shape the head well so it is symmetrical and has a nice final form.

ATTACHING NOSTRILS, EARS, EYES, AND HORN

- Sew the **nostrils** securely to each side of the nose along the folded edge—place each nostril slightly diagonal, as shown in the photos.

- Sew the **ears** to the head.

- Place the **eyes** on the head and sew them down securely with the loose end of color C3—stitch up and down between the stitch parts on the two outermost rounds.

- Finally, if you like, embroider some **eyelashes**.

- Embroider a **mouth**.

- Sew the **horn** to the head. For a small, delicate finish, you can take the loose end and wrap it a few times around the stitching to create a pretty transition between the horn and head.

- Weave in all ends on WS.

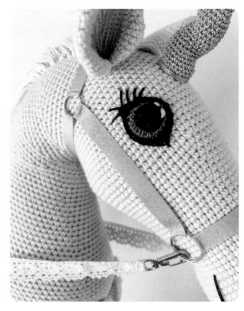

HALTER

Optional

NOTES

- The given measurements are recommendations. You might need to make some slight adjustments to the halter so it will fit your hobbyhorse perfectly.
- The two larger keyrings should be closest to the nose, and the two smaller keyrings should be closest to the ears.
- Make sure that the folds turn in toward the head.

Ribbons 1 and 2 (connecting the large and small keyrings at each side)

- Cut a length of ribbon that is 6¼ in (16 cm) long.
- Fold one end down ¼ in (6 mm).
- Wrap ribbon around one large keyring and stitch through both layers ¹⁄₁₆ in (2 mm) from the fold.
- Fold the other end down ¼ in (6 mm).
- Wrap ribbon around one small keyring and stitch through both layers ¹⁄₁₆ in (2 mm) from the fold. Note that there should be approx. 4¾ in (12 cm) between the two stitching lines (6½ in [16.5 cm] *from the outer edge of each keyring*).

Repeat the above instructions for ribbon 2 on the opposite side.

Ribbon 3 (connecting the two large keyrings over the nose)

- Cut a length of ribbon that is 6¼ in (16 cm) long.
- Fold one end down ¼ in (6 mm).
- Wrap ribbon around one large keyring and stitch through both layers ¹⁄₁₆ in (2 mm) from the fold.
- Fold the other end down ¼ in (6 mm).
- Place the ribbon over the nose and wrap it around the opposite large keyring. Stitch through both layers ¹⁄₁₆ in (2 mm) from the fold. Note that there should be approx. 4¾ in (12 cm) between the two stitching lines.

Ribbon 4 (connecting the two large keyrings under the nose)

- Cut a length of ribbon that is 4 in (10 cm) long.
- Fold one end down ¼ in (6 mm).
- Wrap ribbon around one large keyring and stitch through both layers ¹⁄₁₆ in (2 mm) from the fold.
- Stop here; do not sew down the other end yet.

Ribbon 5 (connecting the two small keyrings going up behind the ears)

- Cut a length of ribbon that is 6¼ in (16 cm) long.
- Fold one end down ¼ in (6 mm).
- Wrap ribbon around one small keyring and stitch through both layers ¹⁄₁₆ in (2 mm) from the fold.
- Fold the other end down ¼ in (6 mm).
- Bring ribbon up behind ears and wrap around the opposite small keyring. Stitch through both layers ¹⁄₁₆ in (2 mm) from the fold. Note that there should be approx. 4¾ in (12 cm) between the two stitching lines.

Ribbon 6 (connecting the two small keyrings going under the neck)

- Cut a length of ribbon that is 8 in (20 cm) long.
- Fold one end down ¼ in (6 mm).
- Wrap ribbon around one small keyring and stitch through both layers ¹⁄₁₆ in (2 mm) from the fold.
- Stop here; do not sew down other end yet.

I recommend that you include ribbon 7 if you are making a regular horse. If you are making a unicorn, skip ribbon 7 and go directly to "Last Steps for Finishing."

Ribbon 7 (connecting the two small keyrings going up in front of the ears)

- Cut a length of ribbon that is 7 in (18 cm) long.
- Fold one end down ¼ in (6 mm).
- Wrap ribbon around one small keyring and stitch through both layers ¹⁄₁₆ in (2 mm) from the fold.
- Fold the other end down ¼ in (6 mm).
- Bring ribbon up in front of the ears and wrap around the opposite small keyring. Stitch through both layers ¹⁄₁₆ in (2 mm) from the fold. Note that there should be approx. 5½ in (14 cm) between the two stitching lines.
- If desired, decorate the ribbon by sewing on beads.

Ribbon 4 Finishing

- Fold the loose end down ¼ in (6 mm).
- Bring ribbon under nose and wrap around the opposite large keyring. Stitch through both layers ¹⁄₁₆ in (2 mm) from the fold. Note that there should be approx. 2½ in (6 cm) between the two stitching lines.

Ribbon 6 Finishing

- Fold the loose end down ¼ in (6 mm).
- Bring ribbon down under neck and wrap around the opposite small keyring. Stitch through both layers ¹⁄₁₆ in (2 mm) from the fold. Note that there should be approx. 6¼ in (16 cm) between the two stitching lines.

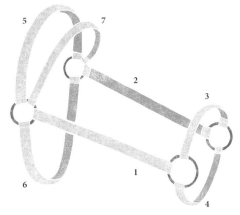

Halter

REINS

Optional

I decided to make reins in a different type of ribbon than that used for the halter, but, of course, it's entirely up to you.

I also decided to make reins that could be removed. Alternatively, you can sew the reins securely to each side of the large keyrings, just like you sewed on the pieces of the halter.

Work as follows:

- Fold down one end of the rein ribbon (*so the raw end is hidden inside the fold*).
- Wrap the rein ribbon around one carabiner clasp and firmly sew ribbon together.
- Repeat these steps on the other end of the rein ribbon around the second carabiner clasp.

PREPARING THE STICK

Cut the stick to 27½ in (70 cm) long.

Place the end cap on one end of the stick.

On the other end of the stick, bore a hole approx. ⅛ in (3 mm) in diameter and about 6 in (15 cm) down from the top of the stick. This hole will be used to sew through when mounting the stick into the head so that it can't be pulled out.

As you're working, if you decide that your stick is too long, you can always remove the end cap and cut a little off that end.

ATTACHING THE BASE AND STICK

The stick is pushed up through the small, crocheted tube in the middle of the base. It should fit neatly so that the hole drilled through the stick sits where the tube ends, at about Round 13 or 14 of the tube.

Now stitch through the hole on the stick and through the stitches on WS of base. Make sure to sew very firmly and around through the stick's hole several times so you are certain that the stitching is strong and will hold up to many hours of play.

JOINING THE HEAD AND BASE

Begin by removing as much fiberfill as necessary from the neck so you can push the stick into it about 6 in (15 cm) deep.

Using the yarn end from the neck, crochet the head and base together with 1 sc in each st, working through both layers. Begin by crocheting about halfway around.

Replace the fiberfill in the neck, packing it in well around the stick.

Now continue joining head and base. Only crochet a bit at a time so you can add extra fiberfill as you work. Remember to add a little extra fiberfill before you crochet the last stitches together.

Do not cut yarn here if you want to add a decorative ruffled edging. If you don't want a decorative edging, cut yarn and fasten off now.

Make an invisible finishing join and weave in ends on WS.

DECORATIVE RUFFLED EDGING

Ch 2 (you will be working on the 78 sc stitches you made to join the Neck to the Base).

Rnd 1: 3 dc in each st (*through both stitch loops*) (234).

Rnd 2: 1 sl st in each st (*through both stitch loops*) (234).

Cut yarn and fasten off.

Make an invisible finishing join and weave in ends on WS.

Ruffles will naturally form by making the 3 dc stitches in each stitch. If you want fewer ruffles, only make 2 dc stitches, or make 4 dc stitches in each stitch to get even more ruffles. If you would like shorter ruffles, make sc stitches instead of dc stitches.

MANE

A full mane needs more yarn than you might think. I used about 75 g Organic Cotton and a little Shiny.

TIP

You can use leftover yarn and sort it by color to make a gradient that flows from one color to the next. For my finished horse, I ended up adding an extra strand of Shiny around every other stitch on each side of the mane.

NOTES

- The mane covers 3 stitches in width. It begins at the ears, goes down the back of the neck, and ends about 4 in (10 cm) from the bottom of the neck.
- Attach three strands of yarn at a time around each stitch.

Begin by cutting a large bundle of yarn strands, each about 19¾ in (50 cm) long.

Attach yarn as follows:

- Take three strands together and fold at middle.
- Insert hook under a stitch (*I inserted the hook vertically down from above the ears and toward the neck*). Grab the three strands at the middle and draw them through, making a loop.
- Hook around the six strands and draw them through the loop; tighten.
- You can decide how thick you want the mane to be. The final thickness will depend on how many strands you attach and how closely together you place them.

Continue adding to the mane until you are satisfied. Then trim the mane so it has a nice, clean edge.

YARN COLOR CODES

Codes with "S" indicate Shiny.

HAIRBAND

Version 1: white unicorn

A: 01 Natural White
B: S White Gold

Version 2: light-yellow unicorn

A: 04 Light Yellow
B: S Gold

Version 3: rainbow

A: 23 Blue
B: 33 Dark Mint Green
C: 05 Yellow
D: 12 Rose
E: 44 Dusty Lavender

Version 4: beaded

A: 01 Natural White
Assortment of beads

MAGIC WAND

Version 1: yellow

A: 09 Mustard
B: 05 Yellow
C: 03 Pale Yellow
D: 01 Natural White
E: S Copper

Version 2: mint

A: 41 Eucalyptus
B: 33 Dark Mint Green
C: 32 Mint Green
D: 01 Natural White
E: S Green

BACKPACK

Version 1: turquoise with name

A: 32 Mint Green
B: 31 Light Mint Green
C (*embroidery*): S Copper
Jacket cord approx. ⅛ in (4 mm)
rust color

Version 2: white with unicorns

A: 17 Warm Light Gray
B: 02 Crème
C1 (*head*): 01 Natural White
C2 (*eyes*): S Black
C3 (*horn*): S Gold
C4 (*mane 1*): 03 Pale Yellow
C5 (*stripes in mane 1*): 05 Yellow
C6 (*mane 2*): 08 Light Rose
C7 (*stripes in mane 2*): 10 Warm
Rose
C8 (*mane 3*): 31 Light Mint Green
C9 (*stripes in mane 3*): 32 Mint
Green
Jacket cord approx. ⅛ in (3 mm)
Natural

**Version 3: light blue with
rainbows**

A: 22 Light Blue
B: 20 Pale Light Blue
C1 (*rainbow color 1*): 44 Dusty
Lavender
C2 (*rainbow color 2*): 23 Blue
C3 (*rainbow color 3*): 33 Dark
Mint Green
C4 (*rainbow color 4*): 05 Yellow
C5 (*rainbow color 5*): 12 Rose
C6 (*sky 1*): 01 Natural White
C7 (*sky 2*): S White
Jacket cord approx. ⅛ in (3 mm)
Natural

Version 4: pink with dragonflies

A: 08 Light Rose
B: 10 Warm Rose
C1 (*body*): S Green
C2 (*wings top*): 32 Mint Green
C3 (*wings bottom*): 33 Dark Mint
Green
C4 (*eyes*): S Black
Jacket cord approx. ⅛ in (3 mm)
Natural

UNICORN WALL
HANGING

A: 46 Linen
B: 01 Natural White
C: S Gold
D: S Black
E1: 20 Pale Light Blue
E2: 24 Dusty Light Blue
E3: 32 Mint Green
E4: 31 Light Mint Green
E5: S White

HAIR SCRUNCHIE

Version 1: white

A1: 01 Natural White
B1: S White Gold

Version 2: dusty rose

A1: 07 Powder
B1: S Rose

Version 3: cream

A1: 03 Pale Yellow
B1: S Gold

PENNANT BANNER

S

A: 05 Yellow
B: S White Gold
C: S Copper

E

A: 03 Pale Yellow
B: S White Gold
C: S Copper

L

A: 01 Natural White
B: S White Gold
C: S Copper

M

A: 46 Linen
B: S White Gold
C: S Copper

A

A: 19 Pale Gray-Violet
B: S White Gold
C: S Copper

PLAY CROWN

Short crown: striped

A1 (*main color 1*): 08 Light Rose
A2 (*main color 2*): 46 Linen
B (*edging*): 09 Mustard
C (*embroidery*): S White Gold
A length of cotton lace ribbon

In this version, Rows 1–2 are crocheted with color A1 and then Rows 3–4 with color A2. Then, you continue by alternating 2 rows in color A1 and 2 rows in color A2, finishing with an edging with color B.

Tall crown: white with beads

A (*main color*): 02 Crème
C (*embroidery*): S Gold
Beads and glitter ribbon

Tall crown: light blue with dragonfly

A (*main color*): 24 Light Ice-Blue
B (*edging*): 25 Dusty Light Blue
C (*embroidery*): S Silver
D (*wings*): S White
E (*legs*): S Copper
Beads, faceted button, and glitter ribbon

COLOR CODES (CONTINUED)

TEALIGHT LANTERN

Version 1: large yellow

A: S White Gold
B: 04 Light Yellow

Version 2: large pink

A: 07 Powder
B: S Rose

Version 3: large mint green

A: 41 Eucalyptus
B: 32 Mint Green

Version 4: small silver blue

A: 22 Light Blue
B: S Silver

Version 5: green and powder

A: S Green
B: 07 Powder

RAINBOW HANGING

Version 1: small yellow

S1: 09 Mustard
S2: 05 Yellow
S3: 04 Light Yellow
S4: 03 Pale Yellow
S5: 01 Natural White
H: S White Gold

Version 2: small pink

S1: 52 Cognac
S2: 16 Dark Dusty Rose
S3: 15 Dusty Rose
S4: 14 Light Dusty Rose
S5: 07 Powder
H: S Gold

Version 3: large rainbow

S1: 44 Dusty Lavender
S2: 19 Pale Gray-Violet
S3: 23 Blue
S4: 22 Light Blue
S5: 33 Dark Mint Green
S6: 32 Mint Green
S7: 06 Dark Yellow
S8: 04 Light Yellow
S9: 10 Warm Rose
S10: 08 Light Rose
H: S Gold

SUN HAT

A: S White Gold
B: 03 Pale Yellow

RAINBOW TAPESTRY

Version 1: pink and yellow

A: 17 Warm Light Gray
B: S White
C: 09 Mustard
D: 12 Rose
E: 05 Yellow
F: 03 Pale Yellow
G: S White Gold

Version 1: rainbow (shown as chart on page 131)

A: 17 Warm Light Gray
B: S White
C: 44 Violet
D: 23 Blue
E: 33 Mint
F: 05 Yellow
G: 12 Rose

PLAY WINGS

Version 1: rose

Center Circle
C1: 09 Mustard
C2: 05 Yellow
C3: 03 Pale Yellow
C4: 01 Natural White
C5: S Copper
Wings
W1: 08 Light Rose
W2: 10 Warm Rose
Edging
E: S Gold
Back
B1: 09 Mustard
B2: S Copper
Cotton canvas in a powder color; wide, soft elastic in a copper color

Version 2: mint

Center
C1: 09 Mustard
C2: 05 Yellow
C3: 03 Pale Yellow
C4: 01 Natural White
C5: S Copper
Wings
W1: 31 Light Mint Green
W2: 33 Dark Mint Green
Edging
E: S Gold
Back
B1: 09 Mustard
B2: S Copper
Linen fabric in a copper color; wide, soft elastic in a copper color

HOBBYHORSE

Head
A: 01 Natural White
Ears
A: 01 Natural White
B: S Gold
Horn
B: S Gold
Eyes
C1: 28 Black
C2: 52 Cognac
C3: S Black
C4: S Copper
C5: 01 Natural White
Mane
D1: 01 Natural White
D2: S Gold

THANK YOU

- To the sweetest models, Selma, Malaika, and Alva.
- To Krea Deluxe for sponsoring the loveliest yarn and for being so easy to work with.
- To Cæcilie for help with styling, etc., and for being the best friend and godmother to Selma.
- To Sisse for capturing all the magic with her camera, as only she can.
- To the patient test knitters, Fie, Stine, Julie, and Pernille.
- To Gro Company for loaning the beautiful dresses.

ABOUT THE AUTHOR

Jeanette Bøgelund Bentzen started crocheting in 2011 and has never looked back. Her background in furniture design and digital design informed her creative design business aircrochet.com. (The name comes from the fact that most designs start with chain stitches, which are called "air masks" in Danish.) She holds workshops in knitting and crochet and offers designs and instruction on Ravelry, at her shop aircrochet.com, and on her social media channels.

www.aircrochet.com | @aircrochet